Hats to Heels

Learn How to Dress to Impress & Still be You

Books by Shelley Sykes

Callum's Cure

Sexy Single & Ready to Mingle

Words of Inspiration

The Happiness Bug

Hats to Heels

Forever Young

The Road to Wealth

Hats to Heels

Learn How to Dress to Impress & Still be You

Shelley Sykes

Sydney • New York • London • Vancouver • Hong Kong • Singapore • Deli • Cape Town

Beautiful Unlimited

A division of Beautiful Unlimited Inc
Sydney, NSW
Australia

For information about special discounts for bulk
purchases, please contact Beautiful Unlimited Press
Special Sales: +61 2 87650270
Or shelley@shelleysykes.com

Cover designed by Roberto Albulario
Typeset by Bookhouse
Distributed by Gary Allen in Australia and New Zealand
Photograph by Tom Koprowski
Printed and bound in Australia by Southwood Press

1 3 5 7 9 10 8 6 4 2

Library of Congress Cataloguing in Publication Data
is available

ISBN 0-9775258-5-6

Style/Fashion/Self-help/Relationships/Psychology/Happiness

Hats to Heels

Style is an Attitude by Appearance.

My mission is to inspire you to create your own
'Attitude by Appearance.'
By sharing my skills, tips and tools I will help you to
Blend your personality, your lifestyle and perhaps your new persona,
For the style that suits & best depicts, who you are now.

Style Sends Signals

With encouragement in the self-esteem department, health and beauty
tips wardrobe sort and shopping surprises
You will laugh and learn about love, luck, looks and lifestyle.

Hats to Heels

Will give you the skills to produce the look that can:

Attract your soul mate

Increase your credibility

Boost your income

Make a statement

Be appropriate

Impress

It's all about Style darlings!

Stylishly yours,

Shelley x

Contents

Foreword

By Collette Dinnigan

From Africa to Australia – fashion, colour and clothes define, whom we are and how we want to feel, behave and be seen.

Shelley will share some of the passion and the skills that that we both experience with fashions and styling. She says and I believe it is true, it is fun and fabulous to communicate through our clothes and be heard by others without opening our mouths, showing us how clothes can determine first impressions. This book is a 'How to' use our appearance to communicate messages and to fill you with glee rather than dread at dressing to impress, whilst still staying you.

I am lucky enough to be able to travel the world and collect some of the styles of the different cultures and blend their glamour to fit the bodies of women. Keeping them feeling and looking fabulous in a style that I truly believe flatters. I love what I do, because I make a difference to people's lives by uplifting the ladies wearing my clothes and boosting their self-esteem, confidence and communication skills.

This book will help you define your own style and allow you to shine and feel fabulous every day and not just on special occasions.

Collette Dinnigan

International Fashion Designer

Hats to Heels

The Look

By the author
Shelley Sykes

Clothes can be so much fun and a great investment.

Clothes are a necessity that can:
- Create your **identity**,
- Reflect your mood,
- Define your **style** and **status**,
- As well as your personality
- Leverage your income

Our image conveys a thousand words.

We can all create and recreate our image as our lifestyle and circumstances change. It's called Personal Branding. Corporate companies spend millions on getting their image right – we need to spend time and effort working on our own image so that we are congruent with, who we have become.

In most cases Stylists are employed – **Corporate styling is big business**, because the value of image is so very important and of course many of our leaders prefer to spend their time creating their magic rather than selecting cut, colour, style of suits, shirts, blouses ...

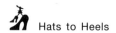

Personality styling has become more acceptable, since more and more people are choosing to trust themselves and choose careers that suit their dreams and aspirations.

Movie stars and music icons have for years relied on **Stylists** to shape their image to suit their personas.

Presidents and their wives, and now CEO's of large companies are realizing the need. **Fashion** Is available to us all as a form of communication.

How do YOU get THE LOOK?

Many people would love to be able to present and dress themselves in their ideal form, but don't always have the skills and flair. I know, because I have been an international stylist for many years. My customer list includes the who's who with movie stars such as Catherine Zeta Jones, sporting heroes and music celebrities. So why not join my A list!

Become your own Stylist & Create the look you need with the tips in Hats to Heels.

As the team at Escada says 'Hats to Heels transcends borders and it's colourful, easy to read language can dress the 'Quiet to the Queens' of this world.'

Become an outstanding dresser!

Let your image speak a thousand words about you!

It's simpler than most people think and very learnable.

Hats to Heels have tips and tools that will help you dress:
- To suit your Body Shape,
- To suit your Personality
- And your Lifestyle
- All Occasions Styling
- Beauty and Health
- Grooming and Etiquette

Other tips in this book will include:
- Property Styling
- Personal Shopping
- Colour Analysis
- Wardrobe planning

Special occasion Styling for the:
- RACES,
- SPECIAL DINNER DANCES,
- CRUISES and
- WEDDINGS

Remember Styling4life is fun.

Shelley Sykes
International Stylist, TV Presenter, Speaker & Author

Shelley Sykes specializes in Love, Luck, Looks and Lifestyle. She is an International Stylist with celebrity clients to die for, owner of the Forever Young Allergy and Anti-Aging Clinics and a TV Presenter, Speaker and Author. As part of one of her TV assignments she had to study Feng Shui. She loved it so much, she became a Master Feng Shui Practitioner and has written articles, books and presented on TV Lifestyle shows. Many of her clients include stars from the sporting and Movie world in the UK, USA, Australia and now Asia.

www.beautifulunlimited.com
www.shelleysykes.com

Chapter 1

It's all about You

🩰 **TIP**

Style is synonymous with success.

**SHELLEY SYKES
THE HAPPINESS GURU**

Being positive and **great in** communication is what this book is about. Why do I say 'great'? Well most of us can communicate, but often the messages we send out are not always what we intend and we can be misinterpreted – a sign of poor communication.

As I have matured, I certainly appreciate more the skills of great communicators and the difficulties many, particularly the young, who have youth on their side yet don't have the tips and tools to apply their looks to their best advantage for better communication. The power of our appearance has so much more bearing than many people realize (93% of communication is non-verbal) and often-older people in their naivety give up looking after their appearance and sabotage their communication powers. We all need to stay connected to feel enough and to feel loved.

I started in the image business at the age of 12 years young, working for grandmother in her Designer Boutique – Langs Gowns at the weekends. My grandmother sold designer Couture. Fashion was part of my heritage. My sister and I were dressed alike in designer made outfits from being toddlers and at 18 years old I was wearing designer labelled dressers and underwear. Mum created her own evening gowns so, I have grown up with a sense that Style and Image is key to communication and glamour so it isn't surprising that Fashion and Style are my passion. The great thing is the skills and tips are learnable.

Today has been a fantastically eclectic communicative day! We are all learning and growing.

I started the day in the gym. Followed by a rose petal bath and pampering. It's understandable to want to look your best, when your next task is to judge sexy young girls in a pageant. Judging the Miss Earth Australia Pageant Contestants – longhaired, long-legged, luscious-lipped, young ladies – a fusion of beauty and brains with a passion for saving our planet. They know that their image can leverage their power to help get the message out to people to take more care of this; our wonderful planet. Mix that with designer dressers, men moguls, environmentalists and entertainers. **Well, it's quite a wake-up call, I can tell you! I will be exercising, detoxing and recycling forever!**

You would think that this one judging duty would be enough excitement for one day. Not so – there was more to come for this Penelope Pitstop! I had to dash across town in my little ol car – a Porsche of course, in time to attend a

Chinese opera at Sydney's famous and beautiful Opera House. Invited by the Chinese Consulate to watch fantastic singers and musicians from all of the states of China perform to a packed audience. It was quite something, with a diverse mix of guests.

I could not wait to get home to write up and share with you the contrasts of fashion and faux parts I had seen in the one day.

To be a model/contestant takes courage. To prepare their skin, hair, nails and body is quite a task. Prancing around in bikinis in front of a row of judges is intimidating. To prepare a speech and remember all the words in a nervous state is quite frightening. These beautiful ladies did exceptionally well.

Being an entertainer is full of its stresses too. Not only do you have to sound great, you need to look great, if you are lucky enough to get picked to perform. Out of 10,000 Chinese applicants 3 had been selected to sing at the Sydney Opera House! Unfortunately for them and the audience, the grooming had been left to chance. Not great when you are representing your country. Hair was dragged back into ponytails with yellow hair bands, wearing a red and black dress is not a good look. 2 of the performers didn't even have make-up on and compared to the professional entertainers with their fantastic costumes and make-up the 3 winners from China looked out of place.

Even some of the models at the pageant found it tough. Many of the models didn't have their shoes matching their costumes ... I was shocked. Some of the girls were tanned and healthy looking and others lard-like. Some were way too thin and some according to my male judging companions had 'unfortunately big bums'. Crikey! What about me? I was glad I wasn't a contestant!

Our image speaks a thousand words.

Let us select the right look for our image.

It really is all about you. When was the last time you really sat down and contemplated how you could spoil yourself and empower the best assets you have; to be the best you can be?

We Write goals at the beginning of the year, but we often see that as a chore of 'what we haven't achieved to date' rather than focusing on **what is right** with ourselves and how we can get the most out of our greatest assets. We can all leverage on our strengths and individuality. Do 'You' really know what your best skills, strengths and vital assets are?

Tiger Woods does, one of the World's best golfers. He never spends time practicing on his weakest golf swings. No, he spends all his time working and strengthening his best shots! Why you may ask? Well his philosophy is why practice on something that he finds hard and boring and only leverages him to 'mediocre.' It doesn't give him the advantage, when by practicing on the swings he finds easy and enjoyable – he can become better and better so that he never has to use the swings he hates. Life is fun and fabulous most of the time for him. It's easy and he makes it look easier.

TIP

Strengthen your strengths and ignore your weaknesses.
That way you will become exceptional and not mediocre.

SHELLEY SYKES

What you find to be fun and easy and how you can portray yourself as you want to be seen; is most likely 'the true you'.

- How do you want to be perceived by friends, family, work associates, partners and children?
- What message do you want to convey about your personality?
- Are you fun to be with, dedicated, loyal and honest, funky or sophisticated or both depending on the event?
- Are you sexy or are you conservative? You can be sexy and sophisticated.
- What is your appearance saying about you – casual, sexy and sporty or are you elegant yet fun, funky yet creative and responsible.
- Sloppy and grunge – give a message too, as does boring and I don't know anyone that purposefully want to look boring and yet so many people do, their personalities are hidden by their attire of blandness or have placed more emphasis on others and let their body health and styling go – to their detriment.

Consider this book a refreshing way to spring clean old habits and create new possibilities for a fresh new or revitalized you!

Honest communication with our-selves is so important in the discovery of our true style.

We do need to ask ourselves the questions listed above twice a year; as the season changes from summer to winter and winter to summer. With fashion sales on the increase, women and men both spend lots of money on clothes yet haven't really thought about their personal message and what their appearance is conveying. Perhaps it hadn't even occurred they were sending out messages. Have you?

Studies at Harvard Business School state and are endorsed by psychologists of the world that we communicate and remember:

- **Spoken words** – verbally by only 7%,
- **Body language** & Tone by 38%
- **Visually** is by far he biggest effect on us by 55%.

'How we say something' has a bigger effect on us and is remembered much more than 'what we say', but the biggest influence in communication is in our appearance – most of our **communication is by looks**.

This means a staggering 93% of our first impression is non-verbal.

It's amazing, it's what we stylists have been saying for years, but now you have the scientifically proven facts!

Let us begin to give our looks, its due attention.

What does your appearance say about you?

It can suddenly feel daunting when you realize that 'how you look' has such a big impact. Following fashion isn't enough to get you by.

Dressing is going to be more fun and easy with our **Hats to Heels** formula, we are going to make it your best asset.

Once you work out where you are on the ladder to style and success then together with my help we can begin to climb the rungs quickly and easily.

In this chapter we need to **uncover how you want to look**, what **your style** is at this stage in your life. Do you want to:-

Attract your soul mate

Increase your credibility

Look sexily attractive for your age

Boost your income

Make a statement

Look Younger

Be appropriate

Impress

Your appearance can help you achieve the desired goal without even opening your mouth.

What are people currently saying about you? Ask your friends and a couple of strangers.

It's a fact people have made a judgement on you before you even speak.

The proverb says 'our image conveys a thousand words'.

When you were a teenager you may have been a 'Punk Rocker with Flowers in your hair,' but now you may be a young executive, an entrepreneurial mum running a business from home or an artist with different skills and passions that still has to sell products to the buyers.

What does Style mean to you?

For me style means grooming, co-ordination, glamour, beauty, appropriateness, communication, communicating who I am, personality, confidence levels, standards and status.

If style is synonymous with success, what is success to you?

For me, I am successful if I am being the best that I can be, for me right now. To be my best, I have to feel good, live in gratitude for what is right in my life, have fun and where possible make a difference to others too.

I realized long ago, that to make a true difference to others is by being congruent in my own life. Being happy being me is so important.

Being nice to yourself really has to come first – as Edward de Bono my friend and mentor says 'it isn't vanity, its key to loving and liking ourselves to the point of 'dignity.'

Have you noticed if you look good you 'feel good?'

If you feel good you have a much better report with people in general and your communication seems to flow in a more positive, uplifting manner.

I realized if I looked good I had more confidence and I was more willing to enter into honest open communication with people. I was freer. Do you know what I mean/

We all realize that we can't please everyone. The most important person in our lives is our-selves. The best way to make a difference to others is by loving our-self and making a difference to our-selves first.

If I am loving and kind to myself then I am sure to be more loving and kind to others. So the most basic and important ingredients for this recipe to success and happiness is to find out what makes us 'FEEL GOOD' and what is 'FUN' to us personally.

I have composed this Style Questionnaire to give you a helping hand. You can download a copy from my website www.shelleysykes.com or www.beautifulunlimited.com.

Let us now help you find out how we can identify your skills and personality by listing all your best attributes.

 HATS TO HEELS STYLE QUESTIONNAIRE
By Shelley Sykes

1. Where are you right now in your life's journey? E.g. parent, author, divorced, asset rich, cash flow poor, happy, excited about future potential, businessperson

_____

_____

_____

_____

_____

2. Circle the type of personality you have?

Outgoing   or   Quietly Confident.

3. What type of personality would you like to have?

_____

4. List things that really interest you?

_____

_____

_____

_____

_____

5. What do you find really easy? Organizing, creative, sports, cooking, design, writing. Parenting, cleaning, strategizing, completing tasks, creating new ideas, networking...

_____

_____

_____

_____

6. What 10 things would you like to do or achieve before you die?

_____

_____

_____

_____

_____

7. Which people do you admire the most and have the highest regard for and why?

_____

_____

_____

_____

8. Whose Style do you like and associate yourself with the most?

_____

_____

_____

_____

9. What appeals to you about their clothes?

_____

_____

_____

_____

10. Could you see yourself wearing those clothes if you had confidence, money & a healthier figure?

_____

_____

_____

_____

11. What do you like about clothes? Image/comfort/fashion or other.

_____

_____

12. How do you want people to see you? Please pick, as many of those qualities that you feel will suit you best.

Friendly	Sophisticated
Casual	Trendy
Smart	Sporty
Younger	Funky
Appropriate	Stylish
Glamorous	Groomed
Powerful	Unique
Older	Organized
Loyal	Approachable
Happy	Cheeky
Serious	Sense of humour
Bright	Down to earth
Subdued	Quietly confident
Loud	Elegant
Bubbly	Fun
Passionate	Enthusiastic
Smiley	Groovy
Relaxed	Calm
Action orientated	respectable
Sexy	Demur
Cheerful	charming
Laid back	conservative
Life of the party	Fun to be around
Sweet	Sensitive
Caring	compassionate
Heartfelt	Spiritual
Motivated	Romantic
Flirtatious	Dedicated
Philanthropist	Studious
Generous	Considerate

13. List all the items and describe how you would have to dress or the colors you would chose to reflect those traits to be seen that way for each quality as best you can...we will help fill in the gaps in the following pages.

_____

_____

_____

_____

_____

_____

_____

14. If you had a magic wand and could change anything about your body, skin, hair what would it be? (Remember we are all beautiful inside and out.)

_____

_____

_____

_____

_____

_____

_____

_____

15. What do you really like about your personality?

_____

_____

_____

_____

_____

_____

_____

16. What do you like about your body, hair, face, smile...?

_____

_____

_____

_____

_____

_____

_____

_____

_____

17. Do you have clothes in your wardrobe you love? List them and say why? Colour, comfort, style, compliments, suitability, do they fit your image?

_____

_____

_____

_____

_____

18. Do you have clothes that you never wear? List them and say why?

_____

_____

_____

_____

_____

19. Do you have clothes that have been worn to death and need replacing or upgrading? Make a list!

_____

_____

_____

_____

_____

The great thing here is that you have just created your new shopping list with questions 8, 9, 10, 11, 13, 17 and 19.

You have also learnt what NOT to get in question number 18.

20. What is your dream life like? Describe it in full . . . clothes, husband, wife or lover, activities, hobbies, social life, holidays, job or profession, number of kids, cars, boats and planes . . .

_____

_____

_____

_____

_____

_____

_____

_____

_____

_____

_____

_____

_____

 Hats to Heels

The most important aspect now that you have a clearer picture of the 'you as you are now', to the 'you that really suits your personality and the dreams you see for yourself.'

Together we will help you to **Dress to impress and still be You** so that you can create the image that best communicates, who you are.

Lets begin our journey together to turn your potential into reality?

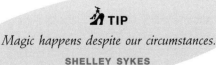

TIP

Magic happens despite our circumstances.
SHELLEY SYKES

A plan of action is always exciting!

We can all do something about our image and style at any age!

Let the games begin!

Chapter 2

Style, Shape & Space

Our image in business or pleasure, whether you are a man or a woman ideally should reflect who you have decided to become, your personality, your masculinity or femininity and ultimately create an image of confidence, capability and have integrity with the type of leadership role you have...

Our personal image is key to who we see ourselves being and who we want to be.

We can create who we want to be at any time. Like Madonna or Kylie, the pop stars, we can change to suit what we want for our lives at any particular time or have several personas as long as they have integrity to who we generally are as a character.

Our personal space is the surrounding we create for our selves, our room, home, office, desk, car, boat, environment in general. It should all be congruent with our style.

These three images, if we are being congruent, should be in harmony.

A businessman/leader needs an image to portray confidence to his clients and his staff.

Police, soldiers anyone who has uniforms set the precedent for an image denoting, protective, capable and team player.

In the first chapter you began to define, who you want to be now. In this chapter we are going to define the 'how' to be you with your body shape, personality and we will work out an action plan to get you to dress with integrity to 'show' the true you.

Like Kylie and Madonna I have had a variety of careers and roles, where my style and image had to change to suit the position, job or the environment.

Working in the travel industry I could wear my bright, light, sunny clothes that suited my out-going personality and the fun industry – still taking into account that I had a position of responsibility. However, working for a 5 star hotel as an entertainment manager I would perhaps have 5 outfits in the one day from tennis gear, bikini and sarong, shorts and shirt, dress and then evening gown. I loved every minute and dressed appropriately for that days activities, meetings or events – a bit like the holiday makers themselves or being on a cruise ship!

B.Sc. Degree
MBA
Diplomas in psychology and councelling

Miss IBM

Panaboard
Sketches by
Douglas Eyre

Working for IBM I had a certain look, it had to be smart, confident, clean cut. Navy suits with white shirts was definitely 'too' masculine for my bubbly personality, so I wore navy suites with a fine pink stripe and had my shirts mix and match; white with pink, pink, pink and navy – Miss IBM.

Working at the beauty clinics the white tunics with gold buttons and a shorter skirt with tanned legs, blonder longer hair and plumped fresh skin and lovely nails and immaculate make-up with a permanent white smile was another look

that was suitable for the industry and yet still suited to who I was – a bubbly compassionate personality that was keen on image and personal health.

As a TV Presenter or actress there is yet another image and persona. This can be tricky though, because once you have worn an outfit and millions of people have seen you on TV it is a challenge to find other outfits so that you don't 'appear' to wear that outfit again for a long time at least. Luckily for me and many other media celebrities, we are able to wear wonderful creations by amazing designers, who are keen to profile their clothes on TV and at events, loaning us their creations. Supportive designers such as Villoni, Diana Regio, Escada, Collette Dinnigan, Lana and many more who use beautiful materials, cut and colour and are very feminine that suit my style and my personality.

For me variety is fun and exciting and as you can imagine my wardrobe is growing, perhaps not as extensive as the Kylie Minogue's and the Madonna's – perhaps not as exotic, but these two ladies are excellent examples of how they can change their image to suit their new music albums, lifestyle and dreams.

We all can.

The important thing is that you have fun and feel fabulously you.

This is where I want you to become leaders and take charge of your image and fulfill your connection with others.

What defines a leader you may ask?

Some one who steps up and takes action despite the odds. They have faith and 'expect' to succeed rather than 'hope' to succeed.

With **expectation to succeed** let us begin with an action plan that helps you get the right style for your body shape and then link that with your personality by selecting different colours, fabrics and accessories.

First we need to get to basics with:

- Colour Analysis
- Body Shape Options
- Style Options
- Summary of Personal Profile

COLOUR ANALYSIS

Many of you have probably heard of **Colour Analysis** and yet still don't really know what it is or many of you will **have had Colour Analysis** and just cannot live with out it and so this will be revision. Hopefully you will learn a very clever and useful tip to craft your style to your advantage.

From my vast experience in the image business knowing your 'colour characteristics' makes a massive difference to your image and how well you look.

Let me explain. Have you ever worn an old jumper or shirt that is not particularly stylish, but you get loads of compliments in the one-day such as:

'Oh you look well,' or

'That jumper looks good on you,' or

'You look great! What have you done to yourself?'

You look at the person giving the compliment as if they are mad, but in truth it probably isn't the jumper it's self that is lifting your skin tone and making you look BRIGHTER, YOUNGER or HEALTHIER, but the **colour** of the jumper.

There are basically two tones we work from in the fashion industry.

1. Blue Tones
2. Yellow Tones

Both blue tones and yellow tones have the same number of colour variations and options from whites to reds to blacks and all the colours of the rainbow in between yet their difference is; one has a much bluer base so the red of the blue toned base will be darker and deeper, whilst the yellow based red would be more a tomato red with yellow and orange brighter tones to it.

Many people have either blue toned skin or yellow toned skin.

Therefore blue toned skinned people suit blue toned colours, which make them look brighter, younger and healthier. If they are blue toned and wear yellow based colours they can look the opposite, jaundiced, older and often drained and this applies to yellow based skin type people wearing blue toned clothes too close to their face.

Wearing the right tone for your skin type is a key factor to your overall image.

This is why colour analysis is great, because it firstly finds which of the two tones you are and then splits it further into two types to be even more atuned to your degree of blue or yellow base.

Some smart person defined them into colours of the season so that we would have an idea what the colour shades would look like and these are:

Yellow Tones	Blue Tones
Spring Shades	Summer Shades
Autumn Shades	Winter Shades

For example I have a yellow-based skin type. I look the best however in Spring shades those are warm, bright strong colours. My mother and sister however are also yellow toned, but their best shades that lift them are Autumn colours.

They can get away with some splash of spring colours, but primarily their best look is Autumn, shades and definitely NOT summer pastels or Winter strong colours.

I bet you are now dying to say well how do I know what my shades are and my tonality. The easiest is to have Colour Analysis done. Check out the website **www.beautifulunlimited.com** under personal styling.

In the mean time open your wardrobe and pick out coloured clothing that you really like and you intuitively know are colours that make you FEEL GOOD. Hold these clothes up to your face and look in the mirror. Does the colour lift your face or do you look tired and drained.

Many people have beautiful clothes. I know women who spend thousands on an outfit and they still look old, frumpy and tired. Yet I know others who could put that outfit on and look great, because of their skin tone and confidence. I also know people who are good little shoppers, who buy a cheap little dress that is the right shape and colour and can look a million dollars.

We need to know what best tone and season type you are so that when we come to sort out your wardrobe, we are picking the right colours as well as the shape to suit your body you so that you can ALWAYS look your best.

INTUITION

Spookily children have a perfect natural instinct to go for their right type of tone and season. In England a group of Child Researchers let a group of 3 to 5 year olds into the Marks and Spencer's store to select their own choice of clothes in the children's department. The kids spookily enough, chose colours and styles they liked. The sizes were wrong, but that didn't matter.

The researchers presumed that the children would go for primary colours (Spring based) but they didn't, many girls and boys chose one type of group from the mix of the summer shades, winter colours, spring and autumn. When their skin tone was checked the children actually had that same tone and season characteristic.

The research was done on older kids, but the results were different. Many of the older children had been influenced by their parent's choice and many picked colours that their parents preferred. For example say the child is winter but the mum is autumn then the mother would select and chose and compliment their child in the autumn colours, because they veered towards that preference for themselves even though the colour did nothing for the child. So the child may have picked burgundy instead of a blue toned red.

The power of influence from an early age is therefore apparent even down to selecting colours. Most of you have been influenced. Some in a negative manner & you are now on a new advertising.

So this is where I ask you to be defiant and pick colours that do suit you and not because you have always worn a certain colour or not chosen a colour, because someone once told you that you don't suit it.

We have all been told on one occasion:

'I like your dress.' or 'I like your suit.'

These types of compliments are saying – like your outfit even though you don't look that great in it.

A compliment worded:

'Gee you look great in that lovely dress!' or 'You look good in that suit!'

Translates into yes you are looking good and the suit/dress compliments you. It's a great suit/dress too.

These are the compliments that you need to be inspired by and that are a true reflection of your success with colour and style to suit you.

From your choice of clothes and colours that have inspired such comments you will be able to check firstly are they **blue** or **yellow based**? You will find that **ALL** the clothes you have picked will be either one tone or the other.

Then you can check which **Season**.

Autumn is easy, because they are the browns, oranges, and greens of Autumn. **Summer** is easy too because they are all the very pastel colours lemon, powder blue, fine pale pink. **Winter** and **Spring** are the bright turquoises, blues, reds and deeper pinks. The difference is the tone. **Spring** is bright and warm – candy pink, lime green, tomato red, cream, whereas **Winter** is white, cerise pink, crimson red and the only season type that has black in it's spectrum. If you are a Winter then you will look good in Black, whereas the other skin tones don't.

Please note these colours are **NOT** what you wear in those times of year. If you are a yellow based, Autumn then you wear Autumn colours all year round. The difference is the material texture and depth of colour.

As a (1) yellow based (2) Spring – I wear bright colours in winter now too. I have cherry red winter suits, candy pink wool dresses and cream wool suits. They look great and reflect my skin type and my happy personality. In summer I may wear cream silk dresses, red shorts, turquoise outfits in crepe. The material and style of outfit determines if it is appropriate for hot or cold weather and not the colour.

Our colour keeps us congruent with our skin tone and looking our brightest, most youthful and vital best.

What are your Colour Characteristics?

COLOUR CHARACTERISTICS

1 Tone _____   2 Season _____

BODY SHAPE OPTIONS

In this next section we have to be super honest with ourselves. These body shapes are to help you RIGHT Now dress appropriately. We are not going on what you want to be or what you used to be RIGHT NOW.

CLOTHING LINE, FABRIC AND PATTERN helps you select the fabrics and shape that will flatter your figure and accentuate the good points.

There are no rights and wrongs, should or shouldn'ts. Most of our body shape is down to genetics and how if we are over weight how and where our body stores its fat reserves. It could be on legs, bums, tums, backs, boobs and/or waist. It just is.

PERSONAL PROFILE

COMPLETE YOUR PERSONAL PROFILE

COLOUR CHARACTERISTICS

1 Tone _____   2 Season _____

FACE SHAPE _____

BODY SHAPE _____

FIGURE POINTS TO EMPHASISE _____

FIGURE POINTS TO AVOID _____

HEIGHT _____   SCALE _____

CAREER/SOCIAL/SPORTING/CASUAL/EVENING PROFILE

1 _____

2 _____

3 _____

4 _____

5 _____

6 _____

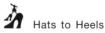
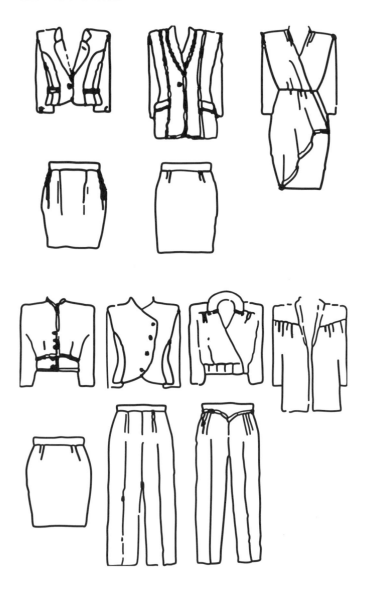

Curved/Hourglass Styles

CURVED/HOURGLASS BODIES

The hourglass figure shape is the classic feminine ideal.

Clothing lines, which have some "curve" suit this type best. These however, should not be too rounded or tight, as this adds unwanted kilos.

Use soft shoulder pads, which slightly straighten and extend the shoulders past the thickest part of the arm, hips or thighs, as this will visually balance the body up and prevent fabric clinging and looking too tight.

Wear details like yokes, waistline shaping and hemlines to accent the good points.

- You can visually wear any skirt length that is in style.
- You should always consider how appropriate it is for the occasion.
- Skirts camouflage better than trousers if you are prone to putting on weight around your stomach area.
- Slacken waistbands and belts if necessary and avoid tight or excessive fabric below the waist.
- Wear fabrics, which give a sense of feeling of softness, which smooth and drape over the curves, portraying a soft line.

CURVED/HOURGLASS with a lean towards pear shape – as above.

CURVED/HOURGLASS with a lean towards ellipse – as above with less emphasis on the waistline.

Heart Shape Styles

HEART SHAPED BODIES

With a heart figure shape, which has a soft graceful outline, the clothes should follow the same soft curves. You should wear shoulder pads, which have been specially designed to help extend the shoulders past the thickest part of the arm. This allows the sleeves to hang un-restricted, or use raglan sleeves to soften and camouflage.

Use designs, which bring the eye to the centre, V or U neckline. Vertical stripes or tucks all make the shoulders look narrower. A high yoke with gathers or a draped bodice make excellent camouflage for the heavy busted person. Yet, I say 'be proud of your bust'. Just ensure that you have a good fitting bra.

You can go to extremes with your hemline – very short and flared to long and flowing. You should always consider how appropriate the look is for the occasion. Stay clear of fabrics, which cling and look too tight. Fabrics, which smooth and drape are for this figure.

HEART with a lean towards hourglass – wear less bulkiness around the hip and thigh area.

HEART with a lean towards angular – as above, may not need shoulder pads and can move between straight and curved.

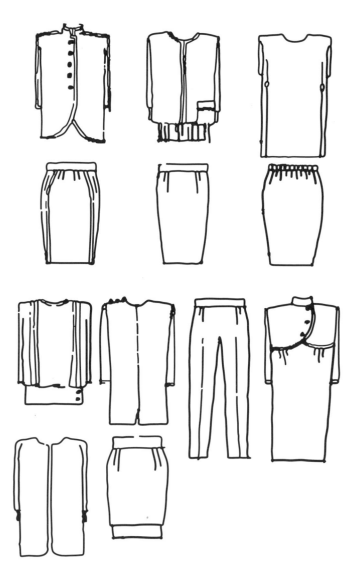

Ellipse Shape

ELLIPSE SHAPED BODIES

Ellipse figure shapes have a little more flexibility and can lean either way. The bustier types usually lean to gently curved necklines and the little to no bust to the gentle straight. Short necks wear necklines and collars low, whilst long necks wear them high.

The shoulders need a lot of attention and you should endeavor to balance them from the front and side views. You will always need shoulder pads to look balanced.

Using designs with straight lines and fabric, which has a gentle flow to it becomes gentle and straight. So do curved designs with fabric, which has a straight look or feel about it. The leaner you are the straighter the line will lean. The more body mass the gentler the line will lean. A straight yoke, wider collars and lapels all help to visually broaden the shoulders.

Wear blouses or dress designs, which take attention away from the waistline and taper to emphasize the hips, thighs or hemline, whichever is the best. The more you are in balance, the briefer your skirt can be.

Many ellipse types will have the flexibility to lean towards the straight figure type or the curvy.

Pear Shape

PEAR SHAPED BODIES

The pear figure shape has soft and straight lines to the body and the clothes should be the same. Always wear designer shoulder pads, which make the shoulders look broader than the thickest part of the body and line designs, which broaden the top half of the body.

Straight yokes, wider collars and lapels are for the pear figure shape. Horizontal lines add width. Hips and thighs need to look narrower. To achieve this visual balance ensure that interest is centered on the bottom half, such as buttons or a centre pleat.

Vertical lines on A-line skirts with buttons down the centre. Jackets, which have a cut-a-way at the hemline, make the skirt look longer. The best waist look is slightly long, as this balances up the low thigh. The best skirt length is between the knees to mid calf.

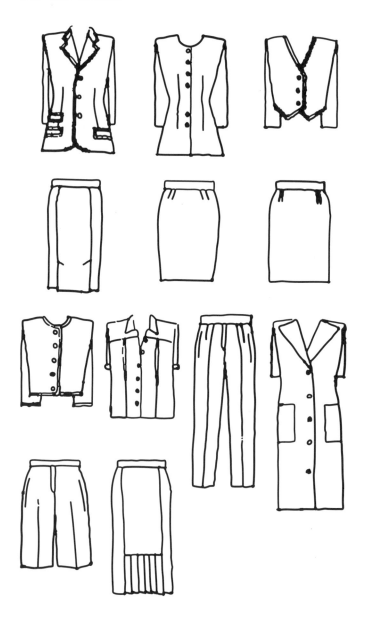

Straight

STRAIGHT SHAPED BODIES

You should endeavor to draw the eye away from the waist, also try to create the illusion of a waist by using shoulder pads to give an extra 1" to 1$^1/_2$" or create a fullness at the top with yokes or epaulettes. Necklines and collars need to be kept straight, in line with the rest of the body.

High or low waisted styles, broad shoulders, unfitted jackets that slope to the waist or just below if you are less than 5'4" to hips or thighs if taller.

The slimmer you are the briefer your skirt can be, but you should always consider the appropriateness of the occasion. Designs and fabric should always have a straight feel about them.

STRAIGHT with a leaning towards pear – as above with a more defined waistline.

STRAIGHT with a leaning towards angular – as above.

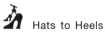

Angular

ANGULAR SHAPED BODIES

The body is angular without curves. Straight clothing lines are a natural extension to your bodyline. Classic shirt, notched collar, long cuffed sleeves. Use fabric and designs, which are straight in line and feel.

Fullness can be worn with horizontal lines at the hip and hemline to offset and balance the width above.

Styles with vertical lines at the top ending in a full skirt, hip line pockets, dropped waists, long waists, which are gently tapered towards the hemline. Skirt lengths can go extreme very short and flared, to long and flowing. The appropriateness of the occasion should always be taken into consideration.

ANGULAR with a leaning towards heart can take softer lines around the face.

ANGULAR with a leaning towards straight – as above.

HIGH NECKLINES FOR LONG TO MEDIUM NECKS
Best suited to face shapes with straight lines

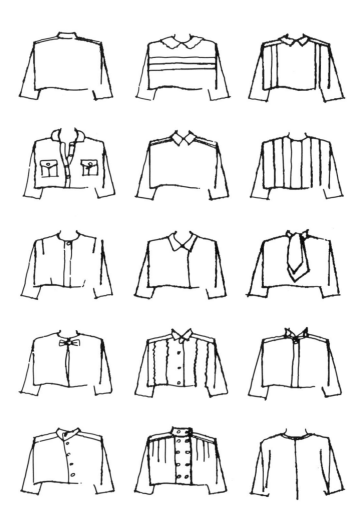

TO CORRECT AND CAMOUFLAGE

- SHORT NECK, DOUBLE CHIN: Wear open or low necklines, or an eye-catching necklace ending half way between neck and bust to create the illusion of length, the necklace then takes the eye. Avoid chokers and chunky necklaces, which cut you up.

- EXTRA LONG NECK: Wear your low necked tops and dresses with a blouse, scarf or short necklace which does not extend below the collar bone, or buy some add on collars like turtle, mandarin etc.

- NARROW SLOPING SHOULDERS: Designer shoulder pads give an immediate result, making the shoulders 1" to $1^1/_2$" wider than your widest part. They make your body more visually balanced.

- EXTRA BROAD SHOULDERS: If broader than the rest of your body, then remove the shoulders pads. Wear collars that point anywhere but at your shoulders. Wear eye-catching earrings, necklaces and lapel clips that bring the eye away from the shoulders.

- HEAVY ARMS: Wear designer shoulder pads, which are designed to continue the shoulders over the thickest part of the arm, allowing the sleeve to hand to be unrestricted.

- THIN ARMS: Drape scarves and stoles. Wear long sleeves, slim bracelets or delicate chain links.

- LITTLE OR NO BUST: Emphasize your shoulders or your waist. Wear a jacket with interesting lapels, or add jewelry to make them interesting. Gathered yokes and bust details – like pockets or a low scalloped collar all add interest.

LOW NECKLINES FOR SHORT TO MEDIUM NECKS
Best suited to face shapes with curved lines

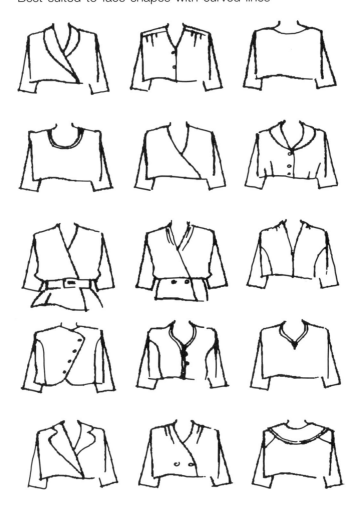

If you have a long neck wear a necklace or scarf to make your neck look shorter

- LARGE LOW BUST: Wear a good quality well fitting bra, which lifts and separates. Also create shoulder interest, or highlight other parts of your body.

- SHORT WAIST: Wearing a belt which picks up one of the prominent colours from your blouse or top will visually balance a short waist.

- THICK WAIST: Wear designer shoulder pads so your shoulders are at least 1" wider than the rest of your body. This will make your shoulders look broader and your waist look slimmer. Wear eye-catching accessories that attract the eye to a more positive part of your body.

- LONG WAIST: Wearing a belt which picks up the prominent color of your skirt will visually brighten your waist.

- VERY PROMINENT STOMACH: (When you look sideways into a mirror it sticks out further than your bust). Avoid waisted designs, or wear loose un-structured jackets, or long cardigans over your dresses and skirts. If you are wearing a belt make it very loose with only the middle centre visible.

- VERY PROMINENT BOTTOM: As prominent stomach.

- FLAT BOTTOM: Take attention away from this area with line design and colour. Wear designer shoulder pads.

- WIDE HIPS. Avoid anything ending at the hip area; end it either higher or lower. Wear your belts slack (pulling in your belt to make your waist look smaller, only makes your hips look bigger)

HIGH NECKLINES FOR LONG TO MEDIUM NECKS
Best suited to face shapes with some curve

- LARGE THIGHS: Wear eye-catching accessories near your face to take the eye away from your thighs. Avoid colour breaks at the thigh area.

- SHORT LEGS: Streamline your legs by wearing shoes, tights and hemline all the same colour. Balance your hemline to show enough leg to give visual balance.

- THIN LEGS: Wide bulky skirts make your legs look thinner, so wearing slimmer skirts is best for you. Stay away from hemline detail. Avoid fancy shoes and contrasts.

- BROAD CALVES – THICK ANKLES: Avoid fancy shoes and contrast colours plus fancy details and hemlines – these are attention grabbers.

- THIN ANKLES: Same as for "Thin legs" and "Broad Calves – Think Ankles"

LOW NECKLINES FOR SHORT TO MEDIUM NECKS
Best suited to face shapes with straight lines

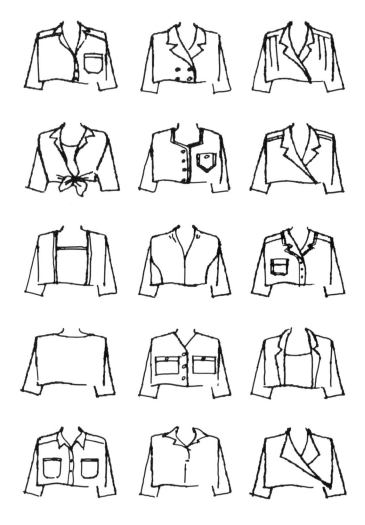

If you have a long neck, wear a necklace or scarf to make your neck look shorter.

GUIDELINES FOR THE 5'4" AND UNDER PERSON
JUST SHORT

Use the same intensity colour for your shoes, hose and hemline. If a colour break is desirable for a change, choose colours which are close in intensity, or which will be carried upwards in a pattern or check design.

Use the following guidelines:

- Always match or tone shoes and hose colours to the hemline to elongate legs.

- Wear colours, which are close in colour value.

- All one colour head to foot (mono)

- Match shoes and hosiery colours to all outside colours of an outfit e.g. coat

- Match shoes and hosiery colours to inside skirt/ blouse/dress top to toe colours. Outside short or long coat can contrast.

- If you want to wear a contrasting jacket, keep it short and close to the waist.

- Wear line designs with vertical lines.

- Wear jackets with a cut-a-way at the hemline. This gives centre interest and a longer look to the skirt.

- Avoid hemline patterns and frills, or any horizontal lines from the waist downwards.

DESIGNS TO MAKE THE 5'4" AND UNDER LOOK TALLER

Note: The illustrations have straight and curvy lines. Choose the designs you like and buy or have them made in fabric and lines to suit your figure, image and what you want to portray – softer more flowing, or straighter more authoritative or a mixture.

AS A SHORT – BIG GIRL

You should always remember a horizontal line, whether created by a color break or a line design is shortening and adds width to your body and attracts attention. Bulky fabric also adds width and can visibly shorten your look, as can skirts, which have a lot of volume or weight in the fabric.

The following suggestions will visibly make your look taller and slimmer:

- Use all one colour, shoes, hose and dress or add a contrast colour at the neckline create a contrasting centre panel or detail with buttons.

- Still keeping shoes, hose skirt and jacket in one of your best neutrals, add a multi coloured blouse in your best basic colours in a lightweight fabric.

- Shoes, hose, dress in the same colour and wear a contrast colour in the jacket, cardigan or coat.

- Wear line designs with vertical lines.

- Wear jackets with a cut-a-way at the hemline, giving centre interest and a longer look to the skirt.

- Balance head size with soft, medium volume hairstyle.

AVOID: Lines that are too curvy
             Too much fullness
             Too many details

STYLE LINES THAT ARE SLIMMING FOR THE LARGER GIRL

YOU ARE TALL AND SLIM

You can visually balance your body with the use of line design and colour. Colour breaks and horizontal lines in the line design, patterns and colour all help to create width. So use horizontal lines in design and fabric.

All the following add shape to this figure:

- Yokes with gathers
- Breast pockets
- Loose crossover designs
- Use shoulder pads to help create a waist
- Bulky fabric for skirts can add width
- Big un-stitched folds from the waistband.

Wear any of the following:

- Double breasted jackets, light to medium neutral hose to create a break in colour between shoes and hemline.
- Separates with a suit look.
- Neutral suit with patterned blouse. Check suit or jacket.
- Wearing multi coloured tops ending at the hip or lower creates one horizontal line adding a belt to pick up the skirt in blouse colour will create another break.
- A pleated, plaid or check skirt with one of its colours taken up into a blouse colour while a second colour can be picked up in the jacket, belt and shoe colour.
- Jackets with a straight hemline give a horizontal line.

- Full soft blouses.

- Large decorative belts.

- Flared skirts.

- Color interest at the neck and hemline.

AVOID: Vertical Lines
             Mono Look
             Clingy designs and fabrics

YOU ARE A TALL–BIG GIRL

You have the advantage of being able to bring more mixes of colour to your look. However, you should still take care not to end one colour and start a contrast colour in a place that you cannot stand to be scrutinized, as this will create more width.

Color and line design draws other people's eyes and grabs their attention. Keep your figure image in mind. Break up the line with hose, wear shoes the same intensity or darker than the hemline. Use contrasting hose in light to medium neutral shades.

Big collars in contrasting colors and centre details. Wear simple styles with enough fabric to allow movement. Remember, too much fullness and bulky fabric will make a large person appear even larger.

(a) Break up your line, by wearing a bright colour combination on the top half. Pick one of the darker colours from the top, and use in a block colour for the bottom.

(b) One-piece dress with a big collar in a contrast colour that extends down the middle.

(c) Big yoked 7/8th jacket which tapers slightly towards the hemline over a contrasting or multi coloured dress or suit will look great.

(d) Jackets with a straight hemline give a horizontal line (it is better to have them slightly curved)

(e) Use diagonal lines.

Drape a scarf over one shoulder, tucking the ends under a belt or pin.

AVOID   Lines that are too curved.
          Too much fullness
          Too many details
          Too clingy.

CLASSIC LOOK

Over the years, one of the most asked questions has been "what is classical?" How do we recognize it, and why is it so desirable in a wardrobe.

First things first. The English dictionary defines classic as:-

1. The highest class, especially in art or literature.

2. Serving as a standard or model of its kind.

3. Adhering to a standard set of rules or principles in the arts or sciences.

4. Characterized by simplicity, balance, regularity and purity of form.

5. Of lasting interest or significance.

6. Continuously in fashion, because of its simple and basic style "a classic day dress"

7. Denoting or relating to a style, in or of the arts, characterized by emotional restraint and conservatism.

So classic from a clothes point of view, is characterized as simple balanced form, regular cut, fit and style, which is not subjected to the fads and dictates of the fashion industry or seasonal changes.

Simple and dignified, fashionable, but **never flashy**.

So to sum it up I would like to add, it is what most people feel comfortable in, and it is the "take you anywhere look." If in doubt, wear classic. It can be dressed up for evening, down for a smart casual look, and it lasts. Therefore it makes the best bet to build a wardrobe around.

MIX AND MATCH

A successful visual effect is achieved by a unified look. A garment or ensemble that has too many points of interest, or too many details competing for attention, does not have visual balance. Here are a few quick lines to help you mix and match your outfits successfully, and create visual harmony with the details on clothes and accessories.

The main pieces of clothing, jackets, skirts and coats, should be chosen because they combine well together in colour and style. Also, thought has to be given to the blouses or sweaters that will create a variety of looks appropriate to the particular life style. Before going shopping, or even sorting out the existing wardrobe, study your figure image, and the best designers of jackets, skirts, blouses etc. for that particular figure image, and the ones that can be worn successfully after camouflage.

Here are a few examples to help you become more aware.

SMALL UNDER 5'4" avoid double-breasted jackets. They chop you off and make you look smaller and add pounds to your "look"

DOUBLE BREASTED JACKET with a skirt that has centre detail, like centre buttons or pleats, does not look in harmony.

SINGLE BREASTED JACKET with buttons in line with the skirt buttons looks right, providing the buttons on your jacket do not fight with the ones on your skirt.

BEST ALL ROUND SUIT JACKET is single-breasted; it goes with most styles of skirts and can be worn with trousers

BLOUSES AND TOPS are a woman's best accessory, they can finish off an outfit, pulling together unmatched jackets and skirts, making them look fashionable and new, also making it look more individual to you. It can change a not so good coloured suit into a unique look.

A selection of solid colours and some patterns in prints and stripes can give you unlimited looks. Long sleeves are the dressiest, and also give a more professional look.

All blouses look and hang better with some form of shoulder pads. In patterned blouses, consider the colour which has to mix and match (jackets and suits).

In plain blouses – buttons that show can be an accessory in colour and design.

Always bring a little colour of the unmatched skirt up to the top half of the body in blouse pattern, jewelry scarf or pocket-handkerchief.

WEARING THE PROPER FIT.

Tight clothes that "gape" and wrinkle magnify your figure faults and make you look heavier than you really are. Just as disastrous are clothes that are too big. When you have the proper fit, your clothes look and feel great – an extension of your body. By having a dressmaker adjust your shoulders, lift your hem, take in a skirt or sleeve to control the fullness, or let out where necessary, your garments can look as though they have been designed with you in mind.

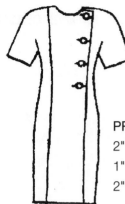

PROPER FIT

2" easy at bust-line

1" to $1^1/_2$": to pinch at waist

2" to 3" pinch at leg crease

WRONG LOOK

Double breasted jacket
With a skirt which has
A centre detail, like
Buttons or plackets.

RIGHT LOOK

Double breasted jacket
with plain skirt

 Hats to Heels

COLOURS AND LINE FOR A FEMININE CLASSIC LOOK

CREATIVE

- Stronger line skirt
- Layers
- Curvy line jackets

ULTRA FEMININE

- Soft flowing lines
- Skirts with movement
- Soft cardigans and shawls

NEUTRALS TO BUILD AROUND

Pastels and light colours:

White, Ivory, Cream, Light Warm Grey, Peach, Apricot, Lavender, Violet

Warm: Pastel Pink

ACCENT COLOURS:

Lilac, Rose Pink, Light Blue Green, Light Periwinkle Blue, Buff, Light Lemon Yellow

COLOURS FOR A CLASSIC FASHIONABLE LOOK

Picking your shades to suit your tones.

Mix: Red with Purple   Violet with Pink
       Blue with Green   Turquoise with Navy
       Teal with Navy   Pink with Navy
       Lime with Navy   Red with Burgundy

Mix with Navy:

| Teal | Turquoise | Green |
| Lime | Pink | Tan |

Mix with Black:

Burgundy	Mahogany	Teal
Brown	Rust	Pumpkin
Tan		

Mix with Red:

| Purple | Burgundy | Dark Green |

Jewel Colours:

Yellow based Pastels – Warm Pink, Light Camel, Buff
Blue based – Silver-platinum, Pink pearls

COLOURS AND LINE FOR A CASUAL CLASSIC LOOK

CASUAL

- A line Skirt plus silhouette
- Pleated skirt
- Burma jacket
- Blazer
- Culottes

SMART CASUAL

- Straight skirt plus silhouette
- Plain classic suit with T-shirt
- Softer silhouette

NEUTRALS TO BUILD A WARDROBE AROUND:

Yellow based: Grey, Navy, Charcoal, Beige, Camel, Brown

Blue based: Grey, Navy, White, Black

ACCENT COLOURS:

White, Ivory, Yellow, Pink Green, Blue, Red

(Remember your tones to suit the skin.)

COLOURS FOR A GLAMOUROUS CLASSIC LOOK

GLAMOUROUS CLASSIC

- Defined line skirts
- Tailored jackets
- Elegant lines – good fit

CREATIVE CLASSIC

- Less defined lines
- Softer look to skirts
- Over scale for easier fit

NEUTRALS TO BUILD AROUND:

Grey	Grey beige	Pine Green
Navy	Brown	Royal Purple
Black	Ivory	

ACCENT COLOURS:

Forest Green, Teal, Mahogany, Burgundy, Red

HOW TO CREATE DIFFERENT LOOKS

A CASUAL CLASSIC LOOK

Add T-shirts and tops to your suits, skirts and trousers. Make use of your blouses; turn them into jackets over a tee shirt. Wear loose or with a soft knot at the waist to give a more nonchalant look (providing your waist can stand it). Replace jackets with waistcoats or cardigans for a softer look. Wear your jackets with trousers, pleated skirts or culottes, T-shirts and scarves. Wear flatter more casual

looking shoes. Swap your clutch bag for a more casual carry all. Gloves in fabric wool or leather. Jewelry less formal.

A GLAMOUROUS CLASSIC LOOK

Change your hairstyle. Wear it up, or add a hairpiece, combs or bands. Wear a dress that has a special touch of quality fabric about it, well tailored for your figure image. A simple coatdress with a satin collar added, or a dress with a halter neck. Wear pearls mixed with a gold or silver chain, brooches and earrings that sparkle, silk camisoles under blouses or jackets that sparkle. Wear evening version of daytime separates in silk. Add a scarf to create a stole or shawl effect over your jacket. Change your court shoes for more feminine sandals. Follow the make-up tips for a glamorous look. Add your most exotic fragrance.

A FEMININE CLASSIC LOOK

Wear softer colours like grey, pink, ivory and camel combinations – or cream and violet add a little lace or velvet. Let your shoulder line have a softer lean and let your fabric have sway or movement and be of lighter or softer feel. Wear your hair in a softer style and your makeup in a lighter more delicate shade. Wear more feminine gloves and jewelry.

A FASHIONABLE LOOK

To create a fashionable look, start to become more aware of the fashion trends in colour and line. Being fashionable does not mean buying a new wardrobe every six months.

It does mean however, mixing your colours a little differently, so look for the new colours coming into the stores. See how they are mixing and matching on their displays, then look at your existing wardrobe and ask yourself What colour do I have to add this season to make my wardrobe look more fashionable and new looking. Investing in a new handkerchief, belt, gloves, scarf or blouse might be all that is needed to make last years wardrobe look revitalized and current.

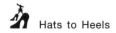

Style Summary

Style Rules:

Style suitability for the occasion and/or personality

Main Rules for everyone:

- Immaculately cut suits,
- Impeccably clean shoes the colour of the trouser or skirt hem line
- Matching the colour of socks or stockings
- Matching belt and handbags
- Accessories are tell tale signs of significance and taste
- Shirts should be crisp
- Blouses for ladies should remain feminine and tailored to fit figure.
- Tie colour and design are key to determine mood and significance
- Colour and tone are very important and you really need to be assessed if you really have doubts.
- Ties are not always necessary to give an air of confidence and style.
- Each outfit needs to be assessed by merit and specific occasion.

See the Beautiful Unlimited website for ideas for PERSONAL & PROPERTY STYLING

www.beautifulunlimited.com.

Chapter 3

Hats Heels Handbags

As location, location, location is to real estate; Hats, Heels and Handbags are to fashion.

If you have a wonderful hat, beautiful shoes and matching bag and belt you can make a cheap dress look a million dollars. Most people however spend a lot on the dress and not as much on their shoes and bags.

Two people side by side, both models; one wearing a dress with matching shoes to the hemline and the other with black strappy sandals, both beautiful – when asked to walk down the catwalk the one with matching shoes visually looks 'better', more beautiful.

Women in general tend to look at peoples shoes. If a man has a lovely suit on, but tatty shoes – it says a lot about the guy. He doesn't care about the small details. He may have lower self-esteem. A man with beautiful designer shoes that are clean and well kept defines the man with taste, high self-esteem and he is capable of taking care of the small things.

How many women do you know have a super outfit on, lovely shoes and then carries their big old favorite black bag that doesn't match their outfit at all? They have everything in it and 'can't be bothered to change to suit their outfit.

Trust me, just like a man not caring – this is the reflection that is projected when bags do not match.

When I was once on holiday in Zimbabwe I was laying by the pool enjoying the afternoon sunshine after an early start. I and everyone else at the pool, noticed a lady walk out onto the terrace. She had a presence. She wore a big beautiful hat to protect her face from the sun and matching beach bag, sandals, swimsuit and sarong. She looked like she had stepped out of a fashion magazine. I admired her elegance and image. I couldn't keep my eyes off her. I watched her walk to a sun lounger and pull out a towel from her bag that also matched her swimsuit. She slipped off her sandals, sarong and then placed her hat under her sun bed. I gasped; this stylish lady must have been 60 years old. Her silver hair was cut into a classical bob. Now I could see despite being slim her skin wasn't as smooth as a young persons, but she was still able to turn heads at 60. I was so impressed.

I made a commitment to myself that I would be like that lady. Stylish and coordinated.

Living in Australia I have the opportunity to go the beach or pool most days. I am lucky I have a selection of bikinis and bags. I have 3 beach bags pink, blue, green, 3 beach towels that match the bags, 3 serongs, swimsuits and bikinis and 3 hats that I wear with these outfits and of course the matching sandals or slip-ons. I too turn heads, because seeing someone look so together and appropriate is 'unusual.' It really shouldn't be like that, but it is.

It is therefore easy to be noticed as someone who cares, someone who will take care of detail and as a person with high self-esteem.

My image communicates; I am bright and bubbly, I have integrity and that I am consistent too. When most people relax and just throw on any swimwear and don't fuss about matching up their towel, hat or heels this is where they suddenly show their lack of consistency.

You may think this is hard work, but it isn't. I know that with the pink bag I have the pink towels. I have a choice of pink bikinis and sarongs and the hat and shoes. I don't have to think about what to wear it is all ready selected. It becomes easier in fact to be co-coordinated than disorganized and look so so much better.

HATS

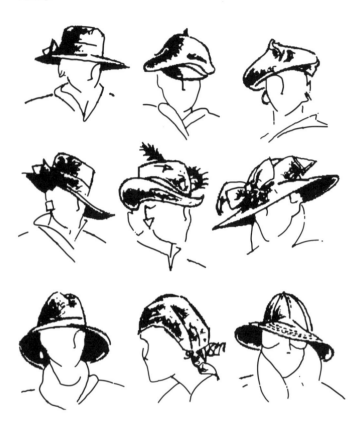

Hats are as much a fashion statement as they are practical or personal taste. There are many people that just won't wear a hat, because of 'hat hair.' Many of us have the phenomena, but the secret is too keep your hat on. Guys can always wet and smooth out their hair. Girls can back comb hair or put it up. The look of a hat is worth wearing.

I have about 50 hats. From bini's, berets, winter classical hats, designer fashion to the sun hats. They don't wear out. You can just save them.

Wearing a hat can be decorative. It can also keep your head warm, dry and shaded from the sun. They can make you look taller or shorter and make your face look broader or slimmer. If it is worn too tightly, a hat can even give you a headache so choose carefully.

The first row of 3 hats have a **straight horizontal angle** and make your **face and chin seem wider**.

The next row of hats are **angled** and will make your **face appear slimmer**.

If your hat **colour blends with your outfit** it will carry the eye upwards. If the size of the hat is visually balanced with the rest of your body (meaning not too big or too small) you will look **taller**.

Alternatively, a hat that **contrasts in colour** to your outfit will make you look **shorter**. A **slightly raised** crown will **give height**, a turban type that fits close to the head will not. A soft type can be worn horizontally, straight or fitted.

Check your visual balance by looking into a long mirror when buying a hat. Also consider the fabric and texture of the garments; you will be wearing with it.

HANDBAGS

Handbags don't have to match your shoes exactly these days, but they do have to tone, contrast or harmonize with the outfit as a whole. Other important considerations are: In what situation will you need a handbag? Will you be carrying a briefcase? Or anything else?

Do you have to carry round everything except the kitchen sink?

Very **structured bags with straight lines** are best for figure types **ellipse and bigger**, not so structured with **gentle straight** lines for figures types **pear shaped**. The **floppy, curvier lines** should be chosen with gentle straight lines for figures types **hour glass** as these go better with your clothes line. Remember to consider the clothesline you are wearing and the overall picture you are trying to create, not forgetting balance and scale.

Just as we change our heels for evening elegant, I change my handbags to suit. **Evening bags** are in general much smaller and more delicate or embellished. I really like all my handbags. Each design being designed for it's own look and beauty.

GLOVES

Gloves complete the look of a well-dressed woman. They can also create a fashion statement. I have leather gloves to suit the winter coats, handbags, hats and heels.

POCKETS AND BELTS

Pockets and belts work like color and line design for attracting attention to specific areas of the body. Make sure that if your pockets are visible, it is on an area of your body, which can stand to be scrutinized. If you have large hips or thighs, you should not have pockets on your hip line unless you have visibly balanced your body, thus eliminating the problem.

Pockets at the bust line also attract attention and exaggerate the bust. This is not so good for the big busted, but fine for the small busted.

Pockets create bulk. They can be used below the waist when you have a figure shape that needs bulk on the bottom half, to balance the heavy top half.

Belts are one accessory that can help you to change the mood of your dress – plain leather for business, fancy and elaborate for a dressier occasion.

Bring the colour of your blouse down to your belt if you are short waited.

Conversely, bring your skirt colour to your belt if you are long waisted.

Once most figure types have corrected their shoulder imbalance, they can wear a neat narrow belt, or a sculptured style. How broad a belt you can wear will largely depend on your scale and the gap you have between your hip bone and your rib cage. Pulling your belt tight to make your waist look smaller, only makes your hips look proportionally longer.

SHOES

I personally just adore shoes and like Jessica Parker in the TV show 'Sex in the City' I too have over 200 pairs of shoes. Each pair matches an outfit or two and of course there has to be the matching bag, belts and hats where appropriate.

For men, watch out because women do check out your shoes. If they are unstylish you lose points, if they are unpolished and scruffy you definitely lose points and they must ideally match the trouser colour.

Two ladies wearing the same dress one wearing un co-ordinated shoes and the other with matching bag and shoes makes heaps of difference to the over all look. The latter just looks more expensive and more together and beautiful.

Accessories can make a cheap outfit look expensive.

Remember that the colour of the shoes should ideally be the same colour as the **hemline** of the dress or trouser and **not** the same colour as the shirt or top.

Your life style will dictate what type of shoes you will need in your wardrobe. Look for good quality leather or suede, as they not only look better, but retain their shape longer than cheap imitations. Above all, you must buy for comfort. No matter how great the shoes look, if they are not comfortable, you won't get the amount of wear you should out of them. Always consider what kind of garment the shoes will be worn with – colour and style – and what sort of conditions you will be wearing them under. A heavy shoe will never look right with a silk or soft looking dress, just as a dress sandal does not go with a serious business suit. Pumps/court shoes in your basic neutrals will go with most suits and dresses.

I am fortunate that I have so many! Imelda Markov the second! I am a good little shopper and tend to buy my good quality shoes in the sales. I noticed a long time ago most friends were spending as much on shoes as me, but always buying the same colour ... either black, brown or navy. They would buy one pair of new black shoes, a black pair of sandals and a pair of black comfortable shoes. 3 pairs in the sales. They would wear those black shoes very regularly until the next sale time so that they had to be 'replaced.'

I on the other hand, bought 3 pairs of shoes or sandles in different colours to wear with certain out fits. They would add to my collection and be worn with pride – a perfect match to yet another outfit or outfits. I couldn't wear them all out, because I had a choice depending on the out fits I wore. Therefore most of my shoes I have had quite a while, but they are still in great condition. At each sale time I would add another colour or style to my collection. I also bought the handbag to match if I liked the style. My goal is to have a beautiful pair of shoes to match each of my outfits. Spookily when we are colour analyzed we find that the chance of our clothes and shoes being a great match with us increases. It's great.

Since I have a list of what I need to complete an outfit, I hardly ever buy for the sake of it. I seem to attract what I need. I may be on holiday and see a beautiful turquoise evening bag that is just perfect for my evening dress. These acquisitions are special because they have a story and are not bought just for the colour, but for their design too and in a wonderful location that adds to the holiday. We do like spending on ourselves even on holiday. For me this is the ideal time to shop and browse – in fact the only time normally.

Later in the book you will be able to list your favorite outfits and see where you can add to them with matching shoes, bags or a hat... or maybe just see where items may need to be replaced.

HANDKERCHIEF

Since fashions seem to rotate every 10 years – similar types of look re-appears using different fabrics and usually with a slight twist. Gloves and handkerchiefs are sometimes a feature.

Just so that you are prepared when they do become a fashionable item, here is the way you can use them to make a visual effect.

Use your handkerchief at your:

- Neckline
- Breast pocket
- Through a brooch
- Add to your sleeve cuff
- Put two together to create added interest

SCARVES

Scarves can make your outfit come together. You can use them to focus the eye on your good positive body points, and away from your negative areas.

Scarves come in many sizes, shapes and fabrics, each one appropriate for a different application. Often adding a few new scarves in the new seasons colors can update your wardrobe. Check the size and shape, and the different ways to wear them before you buy. A knowledgeable salesperson, or an image consultant, can give you personal advice on how to wear your scarves, create many different looks, and also how to keep them in place. Remember your scarf colour and scale has to balance your body type, and the outfit you are wearing.

Your accessories do have to reflect your personality at all times, your mood and the occasion.

GROOMING

Polish your appearance and boost your self-confidence.

Careful attention to details (which are habit forming) is what signals success, professionalism and confidence.

- Hair neat, tidy and in a current style
- Good healthy looking skin
- Make-up well applied and not overdone
- Nails well manicured
- Light fragrance or deodorant
- Hose well fitting with no snags or ladders
- Clothes kept in good state of repair and clean
- No undies showing below skirt or between skirt slit
- No knicker line showing
- Bra straps hidden

Chapter 4

Health & Hair

Without health we cannot enjoy a great lifestyle and the joys of our relationships.

Have you ever noticed that some people look good ALL the time, even when they are feeling sick and others, they can look sick when actually they are feeling well?

Part of being happy and healthy is to look and feel great all the time. Not a bad symptom to have if you're currently one of the ones that look sick when you are healthy!

I must tell you that one of the most alluring and beautiful parts of a person are the eyes. It is said they are the windows to the soul. The eyes themselves never look any older they always seem to have that same colour and sparkle whether a person is 8 or 80 years young. However if we are very sick the whites of our eyes start to show signs of illness. Liver problems – our whites turn yellow, lack of sleep our eyes go blood shot, dehydration and they become less sparkly and dry.

We are all beautiful inside and out, but as we all know that dehydrated skin with funny looking hairs poking out does not look as attractive as smooth, well maintained, plumped out skin. Like a palace, if well maintained it can look new and inviting and the treasures inside a lure, but if left un-maintained it can look much much older and decrepit, smelly and very uninviting. I know that I would prefer to be that well maintained palace.

Some as we have just said; have a natural talent and even a passion about enjoying good health, clothes, style, looking and feeling great.

The good news is that this is a learnable skill. I am dedicating a whole chapter to this area in our lives, because having been involved in the health and beauty industry for the past 17 years I really KNOW how it affects peoples self-esteem and the quality of life.

It's no good looking gorgeous and having no energy, equally its no good looking and feeling less than best. So for those of you who naturally 'get it' and are looking and feeling great this chapter will just be revision, although I have placed some very new and key points that might just give you the edge!

I will spend this time focused on those of you, who really need some help with your health and image.

Like any big break-through it is always the simple things that take us to the next stage. You don't have to be super determined, have will power or a big bank balance to look and feel healthy and happy.

According to David Meyers a leading positive psychologist happy people tend to have 4 main characteristics:

- High self-esteem
- Optimistic
- Out-going personality
- Feeling of control over life

So in this chapter we are going to apply this research to the way we now think and feel particularly in respect to 'feeling that we have control over our life' in fact we are going to be optimistic and state that we know that we can control:

- What we eat,
- How fit we become,
- How deep and well we breath
- How often we exercise
- How we stand and walk
- How we groom ourselves

We have all seen the 'Biggest Loser' weight loss reality show on TV. The contestants are beautiful people in the most abused bodies. We know that they have given up their control.

The three main reasons that they say they are over weight is:

- They put more food in their mouths than they burn up.
- It is a habit and the thought association of self-love.
- Hiding themselves subconsciously believing they are not enough.

We all give up a little control if we are even slightly over weight or not as fit as we know we can be. The good news is that we can all take control back right now, just like the biggest losers do on TV.

I think we can all agree that if the biggest losers can change their thinking and habits we can. It is possible.

After a 90-day program anyone can look and be 10 times fitter, stronger and thinner just taking small steps in the right direction. At the Forever Young Clinics we have had the most amazing results in **weight reduction, energy and vitality increase** not to mention cellulite and wrinkle reduction. It's great isn't it! How you may ask?

www.foreveryoungclinics.com

Secrets to Great Health

Thinking

1. It is proven that our analytical brain controls all our bodily functions. We can control our breathing, it is even possible to control our metabolic rate, blood pressure, heart-beat if we re learn the techniques that some of the monks still exercise, but most times our brain takes

over and does it for us. It has been said that what we think we become. Well start thinking, fit, slim and beautiful every day. It really works. Our brain never wants to be wrong so it starts providing you with the matching body form. Slim, fit, healthy, beautiful and well.

2. The Meta physicians have proven that our water filled bodies are sensitive to thought patterning. Dr Kanoto in Japan has proven that water after being blessed crystallizes differently depending on the naming. Water blessed and named 'love' has beautiful crystals, named 'hate' the water crystallizes in sharp jagged shards.

3. Have you noticed grouchy people are often sickly people and don't live that long?

Be happy and live longer. Think beautiful healthy slim fit thoughts!

Breathing

1. It is a proven fact that deep diagrammatic breathing increases the lymphatic system 16 times. Our lymph carries our toxins and excreta around our bodies from our cells. Some people are like walking sewerage tanks! By breathing much deeper and exhaling hard 6 times a day you can speed up the flow of lymph, since it doesn't have a pump. The lungs work almost like a pump to get the lymph moving so that our cells in our bodies don't end up bathing in it's own excreta and die. [Remember that most cancers are morphed cells triggered by toxins, poisons, and negative thoughts.]

2. Our cells and body stays looking younger and fresher. All cells need oxygen. Breath if you want to look younger!

3. The third benefit of course is that the deep breathing gives us more oxygen, which results in more Energy to do all those things that we find fun.

4. You lose weight over night just by deep diagrammatic breathing, because you end up weeing more and getting rid of the toxins. Drinking water really helps too.

Water

1. I have had a saying for years 'Water in, Weight off'

If you drink 8 x 600 mLs of water a day then you certainly start losing all those extra pounds and help flush out toxic fluids.

2. Bowels, stomach, kidneys, liver stay in good condition as does the skin and the brain.

3. More water equals No more headaches and you stay bright and alert. Your concentration really improves and you literally stay turgid like a well-watered plant, rather than a limp, listless and dehydrated plant. Be a turgid asparagus stem rather than limp and listless or a plump peach rather than a dried out prune. Then drink lots of WATER. 'Happy Love Mineral Water' is packed with high vibrational crystal energy.' Check out the website **www.happywater.com**

Physical fitness

Walking reduces stress and alleviates anger.

Walking tightens bottom muscles and increases ones metabolic rate to burn fat.
Walking up steps reduces fat, improves muscle tone and improves circulation.

By increasing our physical activity we stimulate the body to produce endorphins, which are natural opiates – the bodies natural happiness drug!

When we exercise regularly we feel better, look better and we are better. Feeling stronger with higher self-esteem and all those endorphins why wouldn't you want to exercise?

With MP3 players these days playing your favourite music, the time just swings by and you can really put your body and soul into the movement.

If you really don't feel like walking or the gym is just not you, then try '**Sexercise**'. This type of exercise is excellent for those of you who are serious about getting flat tummies and tight bottoms and want to increase all your endophins for a much better skin complexion and youthful look.

Many of my female clients that had 'gone off sex,' have dived back into it with vigour to get their womanly shapes back – and their husbands are thrilled to be used in their wives physical workout program. It's certainly increased their connection, passion levels and communication as a couple. As the lady gets to look better her self-esteem

returns and she starts to be a lot flirtier and cheekier. It's fun having a great body!

There are other ways of losing inches; I personally think the physical effort or the machines that physically break down cellulite, which we use at Forever Young, are far more effective than the injections that are invasive. It's even better long term than liposuction, because these latter two create waves of fat afterwards if people put on any more weight and they look worse than with just the cellulite that was the initial problem. Do take advice before doing anything invasive that can have long-term effects. Seeing people's bodies after wards is a sure way to give anyone doubts.

Treatment of our outer body for self-esteem and improved sharpness of image is key to a person looking groomed. We have selected a list of treatments that ideally should be done either at home or in a salon of your choice:

Massage helps with lymph drainage
Vitamin & Mineral screening
Regular exercise from yoga, Pilates . . .

Alternative Therapies:

Many people are skeptical about the benefits of "alternative" and holistic therapies. Admittedly many alternative therapies have not been scientifically proven. However, an increasing number of medical practitioners are embracing holistic and alternative therapies. In my experience, reflexology, massage, Reiki, acupuncture, reflexology, homeopathy, and aromatherapy and other holistic therapies have a beneficial effect on the body and the mind.

Din Y San

Yoga

Reflexology

Reiki Massage

Aromatherapy Massage

Crystal Therapy

EMF Electromagnetic Frequency balancing

Le Stone Therapy

Naturopathy

Homeopathy

Feng Shui

Din Y San – Forever Young's Vitamin and Mineral Organ Screening test. This is a machine that gives a person back the control of their life and how to regulate their body energy levels.

People with cancer vibrate at 42 Mega Hertz and someone with flu at 60 MHz. A healthy person vibrates at 70 MHz and so the difference between cancer, flu and being healthy is not that massive, when we are talking energy level frequencies? Since our body is really an energy field full of particles that need certain ingredients to keep the balance in optimal levels, it is our duty to keep those levels in balance. Just like filling a car with the right petrol, oil and water. These ingredients come in the form of water, vitamins, minerals and amino acids. Without these ingredients in the right quantities our body starts to **react**, our energy levels drop, our moods become irrational or we start to have reactions to foods and other substances and our skin and body starts to have side effects such as bloating, itching, headaches, breathing difficulties and we become more susceptible to diseases and cell breakdown.

The Forever Young Din Y San machine tests the body for the persons current energy level, then checks all the vitamin and mineral levels in the body before going onto various food substances, Candida (fungal growths in the stomach and intestines) and other additives now found in most processed foods. There are 88 tests all together, which takes about 1 hour and can be done on children as young as 1 year old.

When our bodies first show signs of missing vitamin and mineral levels the person doesn't feel great, but the doctors often don't have the tools such as a Din Y San to establish what is really wrong. Only if the person's reaction is a skin condition do the doctors recognise that the person is suffering some form of reaction.

I used to be quite plump (up to size 16 dress size) and lost most of my weight in my mid twenties and that was the reason for moving into the health and beauty industry – to spread the word how to lose those kilos quickly and safely. Being over weight was the bane of my life, because

I loved clothes so much and being overweight there are the obvious restrictions – tight and slinky just doesn't look great! Since losing the weight I had lived mainly on microwave frozen dinners and instead of drinking lots of water I had moved onto to drinking 10 cans of diet drink per day. 5 years later, still trim and looking healthy, I started to have mini heart attacks, hot sweats in the night, blackouts and pins and needles in my hands and feet. It was scary. The doctors ran through lots of tests. But couldn't find anything. They told me I had severe stress. They suggested stopping working for 6 months – as if I could and take anti-depressant tablets! I was horrified, because I knew I wasn't overly stressed and that it must be something else. I refused to take the anti-depressant tablets. Whilst explaining my predicament and frustration to one of my clients she told me about a clinician in the next town that used the Din Y San Machine to test the body. It was worth a try. Out of 88 tests only two things were out of balance... I was extremely low on B6 for energy and haemoglobin manufacture for oxygen uptake and the test for Aspartame went off the rectoscale. What was Aspartame? It is a substance placed in all 'diet' drinks, food as a sweetener and preservative. An overdose results in heart attacks, hot sweats, pins and needles in hands and feet and ultimately death. Many people in the USA die of it – like a silent killer, it affects those obese people living on diet drinks and food yet is still eating in excess.

The clinician was shocked that I was drinking 10 cans of diet drink a day. I stopped immediately. Within one week of being tested I started to feel better and my organ test was looking healthy. The organ test, tested all my vital organs from liver, spleen, intestines, lungs... Everything really using the acupressure points very much like reflexology yet extremely accurate and not dependant on the clinician.

One month later I went back to be retested and my energy had returned to optimal high levels and my vitamin and mineral balance was great. I felt brilliant. The clinician warned me that if I had taken the antidepressants and continued to consume the Aspartame filled drinks and food I would surly have died.

Many people are misdiagnosed when the simple formula is getting the right balance of vitamin and minerals.

Without enough **Zinc** a person is **emotional, irrational** and feels as if they are going mad – awful to live with a person with so many mood swings and yet so many people have zinc deficiencies.

Without enough **B2**, **B3** and **B5** a person puts on **lots of weight**, because these are the vitamins needed to help the body breakdown the protein, carbohydrates and fats.

Without enough **B1** and **B6** a person can feel really **tired** and low in energy.

I have created the Sexy Salad that tastes great yet have all the vitamins and minerals that are needed by the body.

Shelley's Sexy Salad

Place all the following ingredients into a plastic large container. Lasts 3 – 4 days for 2 people.

   2 x Bags of Baby Spinach (from supermarket)

   1 x Broccoli

   $^1/_2$ x Cauliflower

   1 x Box Baby Tomatoes

   1 x Handful of Almonds Nuts

   1 x Handful of Grapes

   1 x Red or Yellow Capsicum

TIP

Cut the Broccoli and Cauliflower very small so that they sprinkle finely over the baby Spinach Leaves and are easy to digest. They also look pretty too, green, white and red with the Tomatoes and Capsicum.

The above salad stays fresh, but then you can add different items so that it does not go soggy.

- Mango
- Walnuts
- Tuna Fish
- Paul Neumann's caesar sauce

This salad high in B's, Zine, Magnesium, Vit A, B, C, Potassium packed with the essential vitamin & minerals for great looks + healthy vitality.

I have devised a **Forever Young Detox Plan** for our clients that have problems with their digestion and absorption of healthy foods with all the nutrients.
www.foreveryoungclinics.com

As you can imagine I decided to train on how to use the Din Y San machines so that all my staff at the various clinics could have a tool to help our clients to feel and be great on in the inside as well as beautiful and glowing on the outside.

This is why I am so passionate about **franchising** the Forever Young Clinics around the world so that people can have access to these tests anywhere.

It is recommended to have the whole family tested once every 6 months so that you can keep your energies high and your body weight proportional.

Yoga – is great for stretching, breathing and de-stressing. In yoga practice they teach you about meditation and slowing down the brain activity, bringing some calmness into your life. Many people going to yoga classes believe that it is better to only eat when hungry and abstain every now and again to give their body a rest from digestion and over acid production. Many are vegetarians.

The practices of yoga has many types – my son Rory with cerebral palsy enjoys yoga because he can do it with confidence and at a slow pace without putting pressure on his joints.

Reflexology – is an ancient massage form using the acupressure points of the feet to determine problem areas in the body such as energy blocks or physical issues. It really helps to relax you and gives you a rough guide for determining the areas of the body that are currently struggling. Using essential oils that are absorbed through the skin (most things aren't) the body is able to boost its energy vibrational levels and be realigned. It is great for pain relief.

When I was training to be an aroma-therapist masseuse – my teachers recommended that I take up reflexology to be able to diagnose what was really wrong with clients, who were coming in with bad backs and aches and pains. I really didn't see how touching peoples feet could really work but it was another certificate and I was open-minded to the possibility. So I did the course. On the course we were split into pairs. After undergoing all the theory we had to diagnose one another – first however we had to write down what our ailments were on a piece of paper and hand them to the lecturer. I was fit as a fiddle yet only a few weeks pregnant so wrote that down. My reflexology partner I discovered through the process had 10 ailments according to my tests – I was shocked when each one matched her pre-written list! She could only find one problem with me – she said she thought I had problems with my ovaries or womb! She was, as well as all the class shocked to find out I was pregnant. I became a true believer however when practicing on my niece who was only 2 years old but who continually kept on rubbing her ear and crying a lot. The doctor had told my sister that there was nothing wrong – they couldn't see any wax or blockage despite my sister's gut feeling that there was something wrong with her daughter's ears. As I began to massage her small toes – Amber began to whimper and hold her hand to her ear. I talked to her calmly as I continued to gently apply pressure on her foot pertaining to her ears. My sister and I gasped as we saw golden larva of wax start oozing from Ambers ears! She had had all this gunk pressing inside her ear and it had gone un detected. My sister whisked Amber off to the doctors, who were surprised but who then placed small grommets in her ears to help support her delicate ears and stop the wax build-up.

Reiki Massage – Once again another ancient deep energy boosting massage forms. This amazing technique is applied either hands on the body, which I prefer to do using essential oils or hands off. This type of massage helps re-align the body energies and one definitely feels far more relaxed and calm immediately after the treatment but also more energised and pain free later. I use this technique in all the clinics in combination with the deep tissue G5 massager for extra benefit to the clients that have a deep build up of lactic acid in their muscles particularly on their backs, neck and shoulders. It certainly helps with posture and can work beautifully hand in hand with chiropractors, who click the bones in to place and realign them, whilst we rebalance the muscle and energies in those areas.

The scientist have now proven that our bodies have a magnetic 'aura' that extends from our physical bodies and these auras change colour depending on our health or vibrational energies. Grey is near death, bright yellows and reds are high energy, and lilacs are calm.

Aromatherapy Massage – is a massage using aromatherapy oils. As I have already mentioned aromatherapy oils are absorbed by the bodies skin. They have a high vibrational resonance and help raise the body's energy levels. I believe all massages benefit from using essential oils, because of their uplifting and healing properties.

Even bathing in a bath with 8 drops of pure essential oil can soothe the skin; relax the muscles and the mind. Inhalation is also another great way to absorb essential oils.

Essential oils are the pure extracts of certain plants, flowers and trees. The three wise men who took gifts to baby Jesus were purported to have given him 'gold- an other name for the essential oil 'Sandalwood', Frankincense an essential oil and Myrrh also an expensive essential oil. The best gifts a little prince could receive then and in my opinion now.

Crystal therapy – is another way to rebalance the body and the mind. Differing crystals have differing vibrational frequencies and placed or held close have amazingly wonderful results. The Chinese use Jade as bangles and necklaces for good karma, yet the ancients would have said it was for its healthy purifying vibrational properties to keep away sickness and low energies.

EMF or Electromagnetic Frequency balancing again is very similar to Reiki and clearing of auras. I tried this treatment out and I definitely felt better and calmer. Very much like Reiki without touching.

Le Stone Therapy – I love this as an additional value treatment for the clients having the massage at the clinics. The stones are placed in various places on the back to absorb negative energies and re-align. I also give some of my stressed out clients the stones to hold when they are having facials – to absorb the negative energies and calm them down. The stones are very cool at first touch. When held you would assume that they would warm up to body temperature. If you are healthy and in balance that is exactly what they do. If however you have an imbalance of energies they get very hot to touch. Clients are surprised when I place the rocks on their arm to compare to the feel of in their palms. They really work, yet the clinician has to be careful to wash the stones so that they or the next clients don't pick up on the negative energies.

Homeopathy and Naturopathy – are two therapies that rely on rebalancing the body. Both are great at suggesting herbal alternatives to medication. The homeopath uses minute extracts of plants on the problem that are causing the symptoms. These are given in small does on minute tablet. For example Hepar Sulphate is great to help rebalance hormones in teenagers with acne issues or women pre menstrual. The naturopath tends to suggest plant extracts and herbal remedies that go back centuries and have a great effect on the problem. Both are excellent options to chemical medications and worth pursuing.

Feng Shui – is a way of being and surrounding your life with love and beauty to attract positive energies into your life. It is so cool because the rules and regulations around Feng Shui make sense and 'look great'. It is all about balance, energy flow and your own birth charting – details of your time of birth in relation to the stars and planets and their effect on your body, your mind, the planet and others in your dimension. Scientists are already proving that the weather has an effect on people's health. It makes sense that the moon, sun and gravitational pull all will affect us too.

Feng Shui gives you directions that your head must face when sleeping. If you are an insomniac it could be that your best energy reboots could be in another direction completely to how you are sleeping now. My son was born on my birthday. We are both Leos yet his Feng Shui direction is west and mine for my year of birth is East. We chose our bedrooms for the direction in which our heads would be facing for optimum health.

Try it. Logon to **www.beautifulunlimited.com**

Trust your intuition

Always trust your gut feelings when choosing a therapy, but keep an open mind to the various options available to you, whether they have been scientifically proven or not.

Put together a program that works for you and your children by increasing your sense of health and wellbeing.

Skin Care

Your skin is one of your best assets. Not only can it be attractive but also it has a wonderful function to perform. It keep your body cool, warm and also helps get rid of toxins.

Our skin needs to keep plump and moisturised. In the next chapter we go into great depth how to look after our faces and keep looking great, yet we still need to consider how we can help it do it's functions efficiently. Healthy eating, regular washing to remove the sweat and toxins that are in it, and exfoliation to get rid of dry skin with plenty of moisturiser to protect . . . and to some controversially sunlight! Our bodies need sunshine to keep healthy and in good supply of vitamin D.

Teeth and Nails

If you thought I made a big issue about hair and skin, 'teeth' are my thing.

Our smiles are one of the most enigmatic ways for communicating with others. A smiley person definitely attracts more people and has more friends than those that don't. Why because it is showing the other person that you are interested in them and are open to connect.

Dale Carnegie said that: "You can make more friends in two months by becoming interested in other people than you can in two years by trying to get other people to be interested in you."

I love smiling and I make sure my teeth are in great condition. My dentist, Sam is one of my best friends now. I want the best and travel to have experts work on one of my best assets, my teeth.

The Americans are definitely far more conscious of good teeth than many other countries because they realized years ago the power of the smile.

TIP

Make sure you have a bright white smile and good breath. You'll have a lot more friends and feel happier!

SHELLEY SYKES

We all have had bad breath at some stage during the week. Perhaps it is because we haven't eaten regularly, bacteria build up on the tongue or it could be that spicy meal we had the night before. I carry a toothbrush in the car, at the office and of course at home. People will move closer if you have great breath and step back if you haven't – watch out for the signs.

Hair

Hair can be our crowning glory, that's if we have it. Guys I can sympathise with those of you that, have lost or are losing it. I had my hair burnt off my head once by a hair salon and it was one of the worst experiences of my life. Waking up in a morning with hair laying on my pillow after I got up, or washing the remnants of my hair in the shower and chunks remaining entwined around my fingers!

It's nightmare stuff unless you see the positive. Men that lose their hair have high male hormones and high stamina. Many women love men with shaved heads – they think it is cool and I bet they like the high male testosterone levels!

For those of you with hair take heed of your head. Your hair frames your face and there is nothing nicer than a good haircut and shiny hair.

Hygiene is paramount to increasing your energy and vibration, so guys don't stick more gel on your head instead of washing it – it still will smell and girls don't just stick it in a crunchy when it really needs a wash – wash it. The bounce and the shine will empower you for the day and there is nothing sexier for a guy than a girl with swishy hair – just look at all those hair shampoo and hair colour adds – All the girls swish their hair!

Both men and women use colour in their hair these days. It's great because it can boost your vibrant personality. Colour adds texture, depth and vibrancy. It also allows you to have a change. A summer look versus a winter look, Sassy or sophisticated. Once again it is down to choice and your personality.

I had to laugh when I once did a survey on women's hairstyles. I kept hearing the comment from men that they preferred girls with long hair BUT the comment was that many women cut it off as soon as they got married. It seemed a very general statement to make yet the results from the research showed that within one year of marriage many women did have their long locks cut off. When we asked these ladies why – they said it was for convenience.

It was easier and quicker to manage short, cropped hair. Yet asked why they had kept it long for so long before they surprised themselves by saying 'my boyfriend liked me with long hair'. When asked if they felt sexier with short hair or long hair, they surprisingly said they felt sexier with longer hair.

So what does this tell us?

Even though we a modern society and even though we know to do things for ourselves and not for others, once we find our men ladies, don't give up so quickly on being the feminine attractive girls just for convenience. Divorce is now at it's highest of 50%.

Groom yourself as if still Sexy and Single even when married, because it maintains your own confidence levels, sex appeal and attraction levels.

Most people become unhappy when they have curly hair but want it straight or straight hair and want it to have body, bounce and curl. Red heads want black shiny hair, black haired people love blondes in fact all colours want to have blonde at least for a short while and natural blondes don't know what the fuss is all about.

If we can look after and appreciate our own qualities we will have more joy and happiness.

I can now tell you the gratitude I have that I actually have hair and that it has grown back. Do I condition my hair daily, yes absolutely? Do I use organic colours to be gentler, yes you bet. Do I have a professional cut regularly, with out doubt. Is my hair my crowning glory – yes?

Appreciate what you have wether it is a lot or not, thick or thin, curly or straight, long or short. Make a decision to go with the flow and utilise the best characteristics you have to match the look you want to have for your personality. There are no mistakes in nature. My son Rory (means Red King) has golden red hair and has the personality to match, fiery and bright.

Hair styling plays such a big part of your image:

- Up and neat, smooth & slick – sophisticated
- Spiky or backcombed – funky
- Down & flowing – casual
- Pigtails – Cute

These days you can go from short to long in an hour with these new clip on hair pieces that look so amazingly real and back again. If you want more permanence you can have real hair welded or glued onto your own so that you have long locks whilst your own hair grows. Wigs are far more fun and fabulous these days too. In fact I know some people that wear wigs and ponytail extensions just to suit their outfits for the day.

Anything goes. Just have fun and enjoy being you and experimenting.

Please note however that regrowth of colour still looks 'tacky' and unkept so I do suggest that you always get advice on your colour and maintain it if you have decided to go for it. For those aging and showing lots of whites roots colour definitely makes a person look Younger. The only people that suit 'Salt n Pepper' hair are the winter blue based people, who have a true blend of black and white. The rest of us should ideally colour to hide our grey hairs for as long as possible. We look healthier and younger that way.

Men should also remember to tint their eyebrows if they are becoming grey to keep the whole face in balance with a more youthful look. Most women do this.

Forever Young

Allergy and Anti-Aging Clinics

TOTAL WELLNESS PACKAGE
Includes All 3 Treatments
Normally $390
Special Price only **$300**

1 Vitamin Screening
88 Vitamin & Mineral Tests

2 Cellulite Removal
or Remedial Body Massage

3 Forever Young Anti-Aging
4-in-1 Facial

Book Now: **+61 438 016 622**
For Your Forever Young Total Wellness Package

Feel Energised, **Get** Slimmer
Look Forever Young

Clinics:

North Ryde	Double Bay	Mosman
Specialist Medical Centre	Shop 11, The Promenade	The Medical Centre
1st Floor, 124a Epping Road	The Stamford Plaza, 33 Cross Street	Military Road
North Ryde, NSW 2113	Double Bay, NSW 2128	Mosman, NSW 2088

For Franchising Information Please Visit:
www.foreveryoungclinics.com

Chapter 5

Forever Young Beauty Regime

TIP

Remember we are all beautiful inside and out.

SHELLEY SYKES
THE HAPPINESS GURU

For all of you who are still using soap and water for your faces – I suggest you keep up with the times. The reason we use cleansers and toners is to save our skin working 39 minutes longer per day versus 1 minute, when we use a cleanser to clean the skin and toner to remove any cleanser. Soap cleans the skin, but it removes all the natural oils and dries it out so the skin has to work hard for 20 minutes to rebalance it's self. Washing twice a day for example has our skin working for 40 minutes versus 30 seconds each time with cleansers and toners. By reducing the working time of our skin by 39 mins per day x 7 days per week x 52 weeks in a year, it makes sense if we don't work our skin too hard so that we appear younger or look younger for longer.

There will be those that say oh well I don't use soap or cleansers I just splash with water. This is equally destructive to your skin cells, because every night we excrete uric acid onto our faces (poo) and that needs to be washed off with something stronger than just gorgeous water. When you wake up and kiss your partner before getting up and cleansing your faces ... you are actually kissing one another's poo!

Anti-Aging is the next trillion-dollar industry according to the futurists and Harvard business economists. We know that the power of feeling good about ourselves results in higher self-esteem and increased energy to take more action and do more things in life.

Depressed people or people with low self-esteem do far less in their day than someone happy and energised. The secret is to focus on what is right with our-selves and in our lives.

Extreme surgery has become rife, but I must let you know there are new technological ways that help you remain younger looking for longer combined with a consistent home routine that really does work and is non-invasive.

It goes without saying that stress and holes in the ozone layer cause our skins to dehydrate and blemish much more quickly. It is very important that **we all moisturize**. The issue is with so many cosmetic companies out there stating their products have xyz ingredients that help reduce lines and keep skin plumped, it is hard determining which products actually have enough of that special ingredient that actually makes a difference.

It used to be easy when you could go on price, but now even the most expensive products don't mean that their concentration and potency is any better. Often the price reflects more the costs of the packaging and the marketing campaign and point of sale (department store floor space is exorbitantly expensive, the models for the adds, commercials and R & D all are costed out in to each of those little jars).

There are a few of us that really campaign for and research the products that really do make a difference. Listen, I really want to look younger myself for longer – so why not have a piece of the trillion dollar industry and look great too. Having Anti-Aging and Allergy Clinics certainly helps, because we have the resources to test out the products and see the differences! (Check out **www.foreveryoungclinics.com**).

With modern technology creams have come along way. Creams with high doses of vitamin C and other minerals certainly stimulate ADP and ATP molecules (elastin and collagen) to plump out fine lines and reduce the signs of sun damage and melanin markings. A great cream will also have high doses of humectants to plump and acids to help reduce the layers of dead skin on the surface so that the serums and creams can do their magic.

Forever Young Anti-Aging Non-Invasive Treatments

Although the **real magic is done by machines**; that shorten and thicken the muscles that have begun to droop with wear and tear and the pull of gravity. Many of us have seen people who have had Bels Palsy or strokes where the face muscles have been affected and have dropped dramatically on one side of the face. The people look out of balance and of course their self-esteem drops.

The medical profession devised a machine to shorten and thicken the muscles and put them back into place. It worked! It worked better than they ever imagined because this same machine that put muscles back into place also stimulated these ADP and ATP molecules and plumped out the patient's lines around their eyes and mouths, they lost their double chins and crêpe necks!

The machines are in the next stages of development. Forever Young wanted to keep abreast of the technology in order to get the best results for each client.

These machines in combination with potent creams used at home result in glowing plumped out youthful skin that is firm and kissable! It is a team effort. At Forever Young we devised a way to give the optimum skin treatments in one go and developed the 4-in-1 Facial. Instead of having to choose one of 4 possible treatments all great in their own right we combined the whole lot and charge as if for 1 treatment. The results are amazing skin for men, women and even those with severe blemishes. The clinics are busy. People fly in from different states and from overseas to have these treatments at the Forever Young Clinics.
www.foreveryoungclinics.com

> "Forever Young is how I feel after these amazing treatments."
>
> Catherine J – Film Star

I know some of you will be screaming out – 'what do you think to the 'injections', **Botox**, Restalin, Aqualine?' Whilst some of you are cringing and going oh no!

These Injections are big business for many doctors. I personally have seen people with lumps where before they had fine lines and crevices and the lumps look worse.

I think **frown marks** or scowls can make people look very angry or moody, not good if you really are a bubbly bright happy person. Since the Forever Young 4-in-1 anti-aging facial machines contract muscle and frowns are very contracted muscle, the machines cannot get rid of the frown marks. Botox certainly can relax the muscle and stop the muscle contracting and some filler helps plum out the crease. The result is very noticeable and in some cases well worth the discomfort.

We have all heard the jokes about Botox taking away your smile around the mouth, drooping eyelids and ladies that can hardly blink – well watch out this can happen. I personally think many people have too much Botox applied around their faces and personally I think they look expressionless and so they become in my opinion, less attractive.

In the effort to looking healthier and younger we still need to keep the balance and our power of attraction displaying our personality and character.

Personally I do believe in having unsightly **moles** or big **marks** removed, because they detract people's attention from your eyes and smile. Moles can also grow into malformed cells so it is always a good thing in my opinion

to have them removed even if it is for peace of mind. Here in Australia there are nearly as many skin cancer clinics as there are beauty salons, so do check your skin.

Forever Young Skin Care for WOMEN:

Daily: Cleanse, Tone and Moisturize using serums
           & eye-cream
           Aromatherapy body massage or bath

Weekly: Exfoliation @ Home facial
          Manicure
          Reiki rebalancing massage

Monthly: Eye brow, leg, under arm, bikini wax
          Upper lip wax even if blonde
          Forever Young 4-in-1 Anti-Aging Facial or
          Industrial Deep Tissue Facial
          Pedicure
          Hair cut and coloured

Remember though that we are all beautiful in our own unique ways and having expression lines and showing our emotion on our faces is very alluring and magnetic.

So please use your own discretion. If a physical change will help boost your self-esteem and it's going to be a benefit then do something about it after weighing up all the benefits, the pros and the cons. I think you are beautiful anyway!

Forever Young Skin Care for MEN:

Daily: Cleanse, Tone and Moisturize
            Aromatherapy body massage or
            Aromatherapy bath

Weekly: Exfoliation @ Home facial
            Manicure
            Deep Tissue rebalancing massage

Monthly: Eyebrow and top of cheeks wax
            Eyebrow, ear hair and nose hair trim
            Eyelash tint
            Eyebrow tint if white hairs are appearing
            Back and shoulder wax
            Forever Young 4-in-1 Industrial deep tissue
            facial or Forever Young 4-in-1 Anti-Aging
            Facial
            Reflexology
            Hair cut and possibly coloured

Make-up

Beauty Review Statistics have shown that women wearing make-up get paid more and have the upper edge in promotions than those ladies that don't.

Perhaps it just is, but when we find that we communicate best

- 55% visually versus
- 38% using tone and only
- 7% by the spoken word,

It then is not surprising and makes sense. Image is still key today as it was back in the Egyptian times.

It was Cleopatra that promoted make-up to keep looking young! Make-up was worn by Cleopatra in Egypt, because she did not want to look old. Make-up certainly can hide blemishes and highlight great points such as lips and eyes.

It has been proven that women who wear make-up actually earn 30% more than those that don't. Why? You may say. Apparently if we look after ourselves more and look our best, subconsciously we are sending out a message to our bosses and co-workers that we look after ourselves well and so we will look after others too. Self-esteem is higher and pride in appearance denotes good customer care and positive attitude.

Nail-biters get penalised because it subconsciously denotes they are nervy, low esteem people with reduced self-control.

So I suggest you wear make-up and grow your nails!

I am sure all the make-up manufacturers are glad. It's now a **billion dollar business** so those women that wear makeup, probably they need to earn more to pay for the make-up!

Logically leaders want people with **high self-esteem** and **take care of themselves.**

Make-up when applied correctly can be very effective, it can be used creatively to add glamour and enhance our best assets . . . lips and eyes and of course hide those blotches and bags.

Shelley's MAKE-UP Sequence

- Cleanse – Tone – Moisturize
- Concealer (eyes & sides of nose)
- Foundation
- Translucent Powder
- Blusher (nose, temples, cheeks and chin)
- Eyes

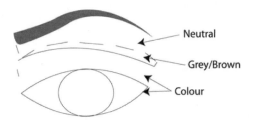

- Eyebrows (slate or brown eye shadow powder)
- Eyeliner
- Mascara (under/over)
- Lip Liner
- Lipstick – tissue – lipstick

Every face is unique. Learn how to apply your make-up for different occasions, to increase your income and chances of a promotion and importantly to feel and look your best.

Day and night make-up can and often should be different to feel and look appropriate.

Shelley in association with FOREVER YOUNG holds seminars and training sessions. Check out www.shelleysykes.com

Contact us if you are interested to come for the next seminar we are holding or if you wish to organize a group.

Cosmetic Solutions

Ancient civilizations down the centuries have seen it's important to adorn their skin and bodies to appear more attractive to one another. Significance has also become related to ones image and appearance.

Today is no different. Youth and beauty, health and well-being are rated the top virtues by most people in our society. Youth and beauty often taking precedence at the risk of health and well-being.

Make up is an ideal way of enhancing a woman's looks – highlighters colouring and adding the illusion of lift to the eyes and cheeks. Lip glosses to enhance the fullness and shine to pouting lips and mascara to thicken and lengthen lashes.

Men too are indulging in cosmetics from creams to moisturize skin to False Body Tanning lotions to give them a healthy glow.

Tattooing

Besides the normal form of decorative tattooing there is the new semi-permanent make-up tattooing that both MEN and WOMEN are having done... eyeliners, lip liner, thickening of fine eyebrows.

Laser for hair removal is very popular, but is painful and can take up to a year of treatments before the hair truly stops growing.

Cosmetic surgery

This is very wide spread and is very effective for so many people. Image is so important in people's lives that if a child or adult has an image issue it can affect, who they become, develop and determine their success levels.

The most popular surgeries are:

- Mole removal
- Eye squints
- Ears pinned back
- Nose reductions
- Facelifts for aging saggy skin
- Liposuction for fat removal
- Tummy tucks
- Penis extensions
- Bust enlargements
- Bust reductions

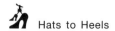

These are some of the most common, but all come at a price emotionally, health wise and financially. Psychologically it is important to discuss any body morphing with a doctor and a friend before this option is considered.

It isn't wrong if it makes you feel good about yourself, but many people find that they still do not feel any better after surgery or alternatively love the feeling and become addicted to having more. **Remember you are beautiful inside and out as you are!**

Chapter 6

Happiness Bug

🎩 TIP

Happiness is an attitude. Magic happens despite our circumstances.

SHELLEY SYKES
THE HAPPINESS GURU

Why you and why now? We have to 'look' happy to 'feel' happy.

If you are ready for a lot more happiness, energy, love and laughter in your life, then this is an extract from my best selling book '*The Happiness Bug*' I co-wrote with Edward de Bono.

There are 9 secrets to Happiness! In this chapter I will reveal them to you…

The psychologists of today state that for many people it takes the first 40 years to get over the first 5! This may be true for me too, but as a small child I must have experienced a lot of happiness in my early days, but then like most teenagers it seemed to vanish throughout my teens and early adulthood only popping up spasmodically. I just couldn't seem to 'get back' that feeling of happiness on a regular basis. Then the '**If only's**' set in. If only, I got into that school, if only I achieved 'A' grades, if only I got that degree, job, dress, man, car, income then I would be happy! Happiness would be mine once again! I seriously searched and tried hard to change myself and control my life in order to get back into that happy carefree state, but it was an up hill struggle being young, with so many restrictions and lack of resources, or so I told myself, circumstances never seemed to be 'just right'.

I really wanted the **Happiness Experience** (back, the feeling of 'being happy' with it's great, cosy, safe, uplifting, energizing and yes addictive ways. You feel great when you are happy, not a care in the world. **Unfortunately, like a thief in the night 'something' or 'someone' happens to you and you're back into that rotten place called 'Ok-ness' or if worse; anger, depression, lethargy and/or frustration.**

Spookily most humans are in these states most days, but not for much longer, because I found **the secret to be happy every day despite life's circumstances** and that is what I am going to share with you now.

Siimon Reynolds the Australian Advertising Genius, says people are like magnets they are attracted to you at the right time and place whether it is to teach a lesson or to learn one.

It wasn't until I became magnetised to the Mr Lateral Thinking Mastermind, Dr Edward De Bono, who having read my inspirational book *'Callum's Cure'* nicknamed me '**The Happiness Guru.**'

Why was I a Happiness Guru? Didn't you have to be old to be a 'Guru'? Edward went on to explain that a 'Guru' is someone, who has the wisdom of experience and has the heart and desire to inspire others with those experiences in order to enlighten anyone ready to listen. The audience are normally people travelling on the same path – so happily that could be you!

Edward had written the book the *'Happiness Purpose'* back in 1979, which explained the value of happiness and how in an ideal world people should and could behave even in adverse conditions in order to stay happy. He suggested I read it, so that I would understand more clearly why he called me 'The Happiness Guru'.

Getting hold of a copy of the *Happiness Purpose* book was the first challenge!

It had gone out of print several years ago, since Edward has written another 65 books since, but as the universe had it, my friend Tad from the National Speakers Association suggested we might find it in the library of the Australian Institute of Management. We were lucky.

I was blown over, when I read his book – I had such affinity with Edward's words of wisdom. It was as if Edward had written a book about my actions and reactions, yet he wrote this book when I was just a young girl. I saw myself nod in agreement to each page. **Tears of joy ran down my face** as the realisation dawned on me that being in a 'happy state' was 'normal' and certainly far healthier.

"If only I had read this book years ago" ... I extolled to Edward, "I would not have worried about being different to other people and I could have enjoyed being me, as I do now far sooner!"

There were so many tips and tools in his book that I had only just learnt. **I could have caught the Happiness Bug so much earlier.** Edward just smiled with his knowing smile and said "Shelley you wouldn't be you, if you hadn't gone through the experiences that you did."

Everything is just perfect – for all of us.

Throughout the centuries, we have all learnt through our predecessors-experiences and their mistakes. I do believe you don't have to experience everything and do the hard yards to learn the lessons. If we did, we wouldn't be able to progress as quickly, if at all. As the old adage says "why re-invent the wheel?" **I certainly want to make your life's journey to happiness so much easier** and less bumpy than my own. Perhaps that is what makes a Guru a great teacher. They have made more mistakes than most and then teach others the smartest, quickest way, for the best results. Yet was I 'ready' to be a Guru?

You may already gather that I am quite a confident lady, yet integrity is one of my main values in life and I was still not comfortable or sure if I qualified to be a 'Guru'. After phoning around a few of my very close friends in different parts of the globe and informing them of Edward's new name for me, I asked them if they could visualize their friend 'Shelley Sykes' as 'The Happiness Guru' too? Their response was unanimous. United gasps of "that's soo you" or "Oh yes", "absolutely darling, your always Miss Happy". These were my friends, who had known me for years through thick and thin. It was all the endorsement I needed to comfortably place 'The Happiness Guru hat' on my head. I was already passionately supporting people with their health, wealth, image, relationships and self-esteem it seemed now only natural to place it under the 'Happiness brolly'.

Health, Wealth and Happiness! It's the name I chose for a TV show I have written and directed and I was so thrilled, when I received an email from Siimon Reynolds saying "you certainly live up to your name "The Happiness Guru" – after interviewing him for the show. It was our very first meeting, which was a wonderful calamity in itself and only lasted 10 minutes. I laughed with joy, because most people would have shrivelled and dug a hole with embarrassment if they had seen what went on that day! The whole interview had been something out of a comedy skit. I felt like a Goldie Horn or a female John Cleese from Faulty Towers, rolled in to one!

My film crew had not been able to make the shoot, so had given me quick lessons in lighting and camera... The appointment had changed both in time and date and then been rescheduled and some how I had a time 30 minutes later than I was expected. Arriving late was not a great start. It took me 20 minutes to set up the lights, the camera on the tripod, whose one leg just kept dropping... Siimon walked in announcing calmly that he had only 10 minutes left for the interview before his next appointment.

I optimistically claimed 'I was ready' as the tripod slipped once again and stated 'that we would be one-take wonders!' as I tightened the tripod leg once again.

The camera was rolling, the lights were bright, the flowers on the desk were positioned in the right place in front of Siimon, I just had to run around the desk and switch from crew to presenter... I informed Siimon what I was going to ask him and suggested the kind of answer that would be ideal... we began.

The first question and the first answer, both were smooth... I excused myself, ran around the table and re ran the movie to check for sound, light and picture quality. Bummer! The lights were casting a shadow. I switched the lights off and ran round the desk.

Action! Question one again, two, three and four! It was a wrap and we finished at the stroke of 11 am – both professionals, both with integrity, both coming from the heart.

I managed to take a few cut-aways as I was leaving the office, Siimon already deep in conversation in his next meeting.

I giggled at the horror my crew or any 'serious' TV or film production team would express, at the whole fiasco – yet I had a great piece of footage from one of Australia's busy billionaires. He too must have enjoyed the humour and fun of it all. It certainly was high energy.

Laugh, you had to or you would cry!

After wearing 'The Happiness Guru' hat for awhile and being in the flow, I realized it would be a pleasure, not a duty to pass on this amazing secret to Happiness, which has been so elusive to me in the past.

I am sure you will be delighted to catch the most contagious bug in the world and never want to get rid of it! But remember the choice is yours. For the sceptics, I suggest you try it and see.

With the genius resource of **Edward De Bono** the creator of lateral thinking by my side, **offering to let me use extracts** from his *Happiness Purpose* **book** in order for you to benefit from his amazing insights, we have found a sure way for you all to catch the Happiness Bug.

Like all bugs some find it much easier and quicker to catch than others. Unlike most conventional bugs those of you who are the most healthy tend to catch it easily, but those of you with a heavy load, toughened by life, first need to unload your baggage, soften up and take a long earned break before the bug sets to work and I'll explain HOW in the following chapters.

Einstein said that 'success comes to those that are persistent in finding new ways, when the old ones don't work.' Be persistent now and read this chapter and let the **Happiness Experience** begin. It is time for you to shine your light, be happy and then make a positive difference to the world and contaminate others around you!

Here's to the best disease ever created for a happy you and a happier world!

1. Have a 'Happy Plan'

Preparation is everything because lets face it when we are 'not feeling' happy then it isn't always easy to think straight or creatively. If we feel down and 'know' that music up lifts us then we can choose to switch on the music and lift us out of our 'down mood'. Once our mood lifts then we can focus on what is right and work out what could be the positive out of our situation. **It's that simple.**

2. Attitude – Smiling

Let's try a practical test. Stand in front of a mirror and smile – looking at your-self whilst smiling, try and attempt to feel sad!

You can't can you? It is impossible to feel sad, whilst you are smiling!

I love to smile. People always smile back – **always!**

Try it next time you are out. Smile at everyone that you pass. You will want to laugh out aloud because it is like magic. Some people even talk to you!

When you are feeling low, one of your action plans could be to put a smile on your face – like an actor. Spookily that smile takes over your body and once again you begin to feel happier!

It is the universal language of a positive greeting for humans globally. Two foreigners may not be able to speak each other's language, but if they smile at one another they assume that each is friendly and open.

Sexy Singles are advised to smile a lot because a smile attracts people to you – that means your soul mate! Most **lucky-in-loves** are much happier than their single counterparts, they live-longer, are healthier and have a higher vibration (it's obvious that it must be the regular sex!) but seriously, their communication and connection is what keeps them buoyant. They are not so self-centred. So smile and attract your happy soul mate for increased vitality and a balanced and passionate sex life. If you need tips get my *Sexy Single and Ready to Mingle* book! It works! We even have a 'Love Attraction' spray to increase your energy vibrational levels so that you can be even more appealing. www.shelleysykes.com

3. Physiology

Our physiology plays a massive part in our attitude, if we stand tall and straight, we feel 'better'. Only when we are slumped do we feel low and down! An easy way to become uplifted in our emotions is by standing tall and smiling. You also look slimmer too – so it's just a must!

Body movement is a sure way to increase your happiness quotient. Depressed people move at a much slower pace and seem to look down a lot. Happy focused people look straight a head and walk with a brisk pace. I'm even known to skip, even at my age! Remember Peter Pan and Tinkerbell never stopped skipping! Who cares what anyone thinks, just do what makes 'you happy" and the world will follow in your footsteps.

I will discuss health and image in more detail in the proceeding chapters, because without your health how can you enjoy your happiness to the full and lets face it most happy people are healthier people too and we will find out how and why.

4. Surround yourself with high-energy People

I personally love to connect with others when I am happy and as we have said happiness is contagious.
When we are around happy people our energy is lifted and we too feel empowered and energised.

Happy people certainly have high-energy vibrational readings. Look at your friends and family. Do they empower you? Are they constantly bringing you down and draining your energies? If they do, move out of home, get new friends... it's time to move on and up! It's harsh reality, but if you stick around 'down people' they end up bringing you down. You can't uplift them for long. **It is my belief that two people coming together should boost one another and become a better whole.**

Some times your family are controlling and have low self-esteem or they fear that you will get hurt if you follow your dreams and don't make it, so they try and dissuade you from trying.

So look around and see which of your friends are supportive and inspirational and start hanging out with those people.

It is an old saying 'show me a man's friends and I will tell you about the man'. The people we mix with define us! We become like the people we associate with. Spooky, but true. Exciting people have exciting friends.

If you want to be happy, hang out with happy people. If you want to be rich and happy, hang out with rich happy people – trust me they do exist! Millions of them!

Mirror what rich, 'happy', people do, say, dress, think and behave like. It can be exciting and fun. There are of course many rich, unhappy people, but they have one difference and that is their attitude or lack of it. Let's face it, there are happy, poor people, who appreciate their life despite their financial restraint and there are very unhappy people who have the same issues who believe if they had more money then they would be happy. The wealthy people who have succeeded financially, who have it all, love, luck, lifestyle and lolly have chosen to appreciate all that they have in their lives and have obviously caught the Happiness Bug. They know it isn't the things in life that make them happy, but their appreciation that they can choose to be happy from within. They are grateful for everything right now and chose to be gentle and loving with themselves and those around them.

5. Ideas – Abundance mentality

Happy people come from an understanding of abundance and not scarcity. The greatest wealth really comes from ideas. Making those ideas come to life. We all have ideas. Only a few act on them.

The ONE difference between a poor man and a wealthy one is LUCK. They say we make our own luck. I believe Luck has four parts:

L – Location

U – Understanding

C – Commitment/Connections/Communication

K – Knowledge

A man with an idea in Uganda may have less opportunity to market or sell his idea than one in Asia...but then gain it might be more appropriate for the idea to be in Uganda. There are many people in Uganda who are extremely wealthy. Location does have an impact on feasibility.

To understand the needs of others and to be able to offer a solution for their benefit is key to success too.

Passion, persistence, commitment to an idea, plan or project and to be able to communicate to others what you have on offer is important too. Its no good having a great idea or product or service if no one knows about it. Your connections or their connections help get that message out. You don't have to do it all on your own.

Finally it comes down to knowledge. You don't need to know everything but you need to know someone who has got that knowledge or where to go to find out. The Internet is the first place people research these days. It is such an amazing tool. Most wealthy people rate their team as the highest resource they have. John Paul Getty one of the wealthiest men in the US last century stated he would rather have 100 people working for him than commit 100 hours of his own time that could best be utilised thinking up new ideas.

Siimon Reynolds one of Australia's richest men says that to have a great business you need:

- Financial backing
- A great support team
- A great idea or business plan

When I personally started to research other successful people, I realised that **no one had done it on their own**. They had all both had a mentor or a financial backer or someone who believed in their dream or idea and given them a lift up the ladder.

I read the *One Minute Millionaire* by Jack Cranfield, whom suggested that we all need to go out and find a millionaire as a mentor to help us develop our millionaire strategies. I was lucky. I had been introduced to a 'billionaire' who found millions 'boring'! He was a 68-year-old Yorkshire man that had moved to Australia as a young man. After struggling in Tasmania in the property market, he sought to make his wealth in Sydney and arrived with only $50. He loved property and to negotiate. He found a property that needed renovation and then sat by a phone and rang every banker, financier in town until he found one that loved his idea, passion and zest to renovate and sell to a different clientele.

Offering a 50% return on his investment Bernard Lewis began his climb to the top of Australian property league. His advice to me before he died was not to worry about what percentage of your idea you were giving away or sharing, but to get it into motion. When your idea works people start wanting to throw money at your next ideas, projects and plans and there are always more ideas, projects and plans to follow the first.

His sound advice seems to ricochet with so many successful people.

Walt Disney as we all know, had one of the biggest, best, most exciting ideas and with only $5 left in his pocket he continued to knock on the doors of the big investors, not accepting rejection personally, he persisted until one man finally agreed to finance his dream project Disney land, which then became a reality for us all.

Richard Branson is one of the richest men in the world and I believe from meeting him, one of the happiest. He lives in gratitude and appreciates all that he has created. He is aware of the power that his possessions bring and uses that power in the force for good. He is a great philanthropist and takes pleasure in helping others achieve their dreams, whilst still following his own. He is definitely a people's person and realizes his strength is in his people and the people around the world.

He still loves the challenges life throws at him and understands life is a constant lesson. I was thrilled to see his zest for life and his humbleness. A great man we can all emulate and look up to because he is truly being himself for himself. He is shining his light and allowing others to do the same.

6. Live in the Now

There is a saying that the past is long gone, tomorrow is an unknown future, but **the present is the gift that can be enjoyed right now**. I love gifts. 'Right now' is so very special – it is life. Just stop for a moment and just savour this moment... you are obviously reading this book... where are you, are you comfortable, somewhere lovely and exotic or curled up in bed at home, lying next to someone – so give them a kiss?

I am lying in bed; it's 10 am – what luxury, with my laptop rested against my knees in my Princess Shelley bed plumped up with a heap of pretty cushions. I have sunshine beaming through my windows, blue skies, the scent from the flowers in the vase facing my bed is filling the room with a delicious sweet aroma, my son's computer is zapping and crashing in the distant back ground and I am feeling happy and content as the words just spill out on to this page. I feel lucky I have this time right now to type before the 'normal routine begins' – all is well, at peace, safe and exciting, because I know that this book will touch you in some inspirational way.

Worry leads to fear and the fear of possibilities is more frightening than facing the thing we are worrying about. As the song says:

"Don't worry, be happy"

It has become a habit for many of us to worry, because our parents have taught us and we hear it time and time again... I worry about you... I'm worried about the...

TIP

Worry is the most useless, ineffective waste of our gift, our present time.

SHELLEY SYKES

The present is all we have right now. **So happy people just focus on right now and experience the joy that this moment is bringing.**

Does it matter right now as you are reading this book if you have millions in the bank or not? No.

Does it matter as you are reading this book if you have found your soul mate or not? No.

Does it matter if right now if you are a little over weight, spotty, too thin, can't afford a 'thingy-magig' or not? No.

Right now you are enjoying down time for yourself. You are investing in yourself so that you can enjoy more of the happy you and by being the happy you, make a difference to others. How exciting is that!

By being present you can appreciate the people, the place, the experiences and the journey right now as it is. Right now my environment could be like that of Jackie Collins equivalent, in her mansion in Hollywood writing her next best seller – at the other side of the world here I am luxuriating in opulence writing a world best seller soul touching stuff that's easy to read like Jackie's sexy stuff.

Ok so I don't have her maids making lunch downstairs, but I'm not hungry at the moment. I don't have her millions in the bank, but who needs millions to do what I am doing right now – writing. So back to my 'Happy Present' this glamorous writer, me laying in the princess bed, typing, whilst my son is happily kept busy on his computer, the flowers continue to fill the air in my designer, immaculately clean apartment and whilst the sun continues to shine through my windows ... it's glorious!

7. Expect the best

A happy habit that is just a must is to expect the best. Some people think that that will bring bad karma or it is tempting fate. If you are not happy most of the time and you want to be, then change and expect the best from now on. A common factor between highly successful happy people is they expect to win, succeed, be happy, be the best at what they do, achieve their goal, be lucky ... it just is.

I tell everyone I am one of the luckiest people I know. I have had some amazing things happen to me in my life – just the people that I get to meet is pretty awesome and lucky really, to travel to places like the Antarctica on a cruise ship is pretty lucky, to swim in volcanoes and live in a place where the parrots live freely and not in cages is pretty cool.

In fact, however if you count up all the 'unlucky' things that have ever happened to me I am probably one of the most un-luckiest people I have ever met too. Car crashes, divorce, disabled child, major financial loss, sickness, near death experiences...

Most successful people have had more failures than most people. Why? Because they try more things and go for what ever they are aiming for. If you think you will succeed, you go for it. If you don't expect to succeed why try at all? Most people don't even begin to try. Remember Thomas Edison who invented the light bulb. It took 10,000 experiments before it finally worked. He did it! Most unsuccessful people would have quit. If you quit you are guaranteed to fail. If you persist you are guaranteed an interesting journey.

Remember it is better to try and fail than not try at all and live in regret. If you expect the best then of course you are going to embark on a new adventure and see where it takes you. It's a numbers game and in the end you come up smelling of roses a winner! Nothing ventured is ever wrong. Taking the risk in a venture is quite a ride.

8. Focus on being Successful

Happy people are definitely focused. Wether it is to be a loving partner, parent, a mother or a business man on a mission to make a difference to how people think, work, do things, enjoy themselves or whole combinations of things.

Our dreams are what make us unique and literally shine our light. It is called living in the flame. It is that 'je ne sais pas' as the French say, 'I don't know what' that ignites us up and on. A passion to be or do something that excites us inside. It is different for each one of us. It is a dream, an idea or way of being that suits our personality and us from the core rather than has been imposed upon us.

People's success is measured by their own interpretation of what success is. I know a man who says he is successful when he wakes up every morning and he is alive and well. Just to be above ground is success in his eyes. This man is easily pleased and finds success easily to come by each and every day. Mark is one of the happiest men I know.

There are others who have such high standards of success that they only feel success occasionally. One man, who became a client, said that he only felt successful when each of his employees asks for his help. This is a man with 600 employees, millions in the bank, great wife, kids, holidays, great business, but this man feels unsuccessful because not all his employees asks for his help!

Lets face it, most would avoid asking for the CEO's help just so that they don't look incompetent or not enough for their job. After working out a better success plan this man's whole persona has shifted. He lives in gratitude with all the things that are going right in his life. The weight of the world has lifted from his shoulders and he is a lot jollier. His new success model is that he feels successful when his staff 'doesn't ask' for help, because it means that they are all working well. He still has an open door policy so that they can come to him with their questions and ideas, because he realises he likes to help people and make a difference. So to allow for that we implemented a plan to help his local community by setting up a tithing scheme through 2b1 charitable Foundation for the company and employees if they wanted to join in making a difference to individuals and groups in their region.

If you notice, nothing really changed in his life except the meaning he was giving to things. When the meaning changes in a way that up lifts you, then it can only motivate and inspire you. Good things can then come from this newfound energy and inspiration, such as his company contribution charity fund. I bet he is now much easier to live with and work with. Have you noticed unhappy people are a lot grouchier than happy people?

9. Shine

Nelson Mandela told us 'who are we not to shine our light!' Sometimes the battle isn't about shining, but just finding the light bulb and the switch. If you don't know what your purpose in life is or what your special gifts are how then do you know how to shine?

To some people it is so obvious and to others it is a burden and torment working it out. **Simply put, to shine is to be just who we are and do what we really enjoy being and doing and somehow that magic combination works and inspires others.**

It really is that simple. Truly.

Some say that you need to have grandiose ideas, plans to change the world, but no, that is not true for everyone. Our purpose is JUST TO BE. Being a happy bee is much better than a grumpy bee. We often put restrictions on ourselves such as I will only go to the beach when I have finished this chapter...not me if I feel I need to go, I go now, whilst the weather is sunny and I will benefit from the fresh air. I can always come back and type into the night and finish off the chapter when the beach is cold and black.

It's not about doing the right thing for others. It's about doing the right thing for us. We touch and inspire others by being genuine and ourselves.

It took me ages to find it out. After years of trying to please people, being the good girl it never seemed to fully work.

I think the easiest way to shine is to just follow your heart and your gut. Forget logic and your head. If you follow your instincts then the journey will be a much freer experience and more fun. It is certainly easier to be happier when you have to only work out how to keep yourself jolly.

Nelson Mandela was a prisoner in jail for 27 years just for a belief that black and white people should be treated equally. One man locked away. He would not give up his dream and whilst in prison he stayed happy and expectant because he was being true to himself. It would have been more logical and easier on his family if he had conceded his beliefs, but no, he did it for himself and the result was awesome. When released he was not bitter and twisted. He expected that his dream would become a reality somehow, some day. He probably never dreamed that one day he would become president of his country or a world leader.

Sometimes our dreams become even bigger better realities than we could ever have envisioned.

When Richard Branson first started his Virgin Record Shop he probably never envisioned owning airlines, credit cards and a multitude of other global businesses. He was just doing and being himself, playing records in a place with comfy chairs.

The answer to 'how do I shine is':

BE YOURSELF and DO what makes you feel happy even when the chips are down.

Chapter 7

Lucky-in-Love or Sexy Single?

Lucky-in-Loves were once **Sexy Singles**. It doesn't mean that they are not sexy. Now they are hopefully Sexy and Lucky-in-Love.

Many **Sexy Singles** definitely spend more on clothes and take more care of their appearance in general. **Sexy Singles** still want to attract their partner and probably impress people at work. They are definitely on a mission to communicate messages. **Lucky-in-Loves** can become complacent and that isn't good either with 50% of marriages breaking up. Job security no longer exists, marrieds' still need to look groomed and styled even at work.

We are all put on notice that we need to continue to make efforts to look, feel and be attractive and send out correct messages such as:

- We love ourselves so others can love us too.
- We have high self-esteem.
- We are efficient and proficient.
- We are capable and appropriate.
- We are loving and caring.
- We are organised and enough.
- We are sexy and lovable.

I know **Sexy Singles** that have dull clothes for work and then sexy beautiful clothes for social. People at work would never recognise them when they are out. This is not being congruent and also limits that person's chances of meeting the love of their life at work, where according to statistics show 50% of people meet their future spouses at work.

We have already pointed out that many new brides chop off their hair within one year of being married; to their partners dismay. All in the name of convenience – let us break this habit of suddenly being less.

The importance here is feeling the same sexy stylish you whether you have found your partner or not.

How you dress definitely indicates the type of person that you are going to attract. If you are dressing one way, but wanting to attract a person who will most likely be attracted to a different look you are going to be crossing wires.

Men definitely are distinct in the types of women they like and are very visual. In my book '*Sexy Single & Ready to*

Mingle' I co-wrote with Edward de Bono we related men to dogs liking different breeds from intelligent poodles to bimbo Afghan hounds...men in general always seem to have a particular type of breed they date or marry.

Women on the other hand are attracted to a mongrel. A man with many contributes. The best of all the breeds!

The best way to attract your ideal man is to be the best you can be – being you. **That means dressing to enhance all your best attributes, highlighting your personality and femininity. Being congruent and appropriate. Wearing your best every day.**

I love all my clothes and the way they look – especially those that I got for a bargain in the sale.

Your energies and vibration is so much higher when you are '**being you**.' The happy true you magnetizes people into your life that like your look and energy.

So if you have got this right, it doesn't mean shortening your skirts and lowering your tops just to get a man's attention. It means wearing outfits that make YOU feel sexy and desirable and appropriate wearing.

One of my best assets besides my smile is my boobs, small waist and legs. So I wear clothes that accentuate my figure, out-in-out. I wear feminine clothes in my Spring tones and I love high heels to show off my shapely legs. Yes in winter I wear stockings and suspender belt. But I don't wear them to be sexy at the sake of having bumps show through on my skirts.

In fact I prefer summer so that I don't have to wear stockings. I love wearing less rather than more – yet I am aware that we have to be appropriate. The variety keeps me enthused about clothes and the reactions. I love variety, yet with my busy schedule I like some consistency. I really know what I feel sexy in. I like most of my clothes to look sexy and feminine even if it is a suit. Just the cut and colour, fabric and the flow when I walk can be beautiful.

This chapter is a wake up call for any of you who have become too complacent or have become a martyr and spoil other family members leaving yourself last – like Cinderella.

Well Ping! It's now your time to do what you need to do to live your life and do what you want to do.

As a mother I never have worn baggy 'tracky' pants – No it was just as easy to slip on a pretty dress and slip on some shoes or in winter some smart trousers and jumper and boots with some lipstick. It's all quick and easy if you have your wardrobe organised with clothes that suit you.

Now this doesn't mean that you need to go out shopping every week for new stuff – no. What it does mean is that what we want to do is create that great feeling every time you put on clothes. Your clothes have to look, feel and mean something special to you for your own dignity and self-esteem. Certain items in your wardrobe when you put them on make you feel 'great' no matter how long you have had them. These types of outfits are the sorts that should be filling your wardrobe and that you should be wearing on a daily basis.

Remember that our goal is to be a **Sexy Lucky-in-Love**!

Chapter 8

In the Bedroom

It has been proven that by dressing up we actually feel more empowered. Don't you just love it when you are freshly showered and you put on new underwear and then your new clothes and new shoes? You actually feel new and energised. It feels great to know everything looks good on every level…

Putting the same new clothes on with old underwear just doesn't feel the same. Or putting on new shoes with old socks takes away from the splendour of having 'nice stuff' on all the levels. No one else can tell looking at you that you have old daggy underwear or old socks but YOU KNOW and it changes the feeling.

> "Be a yardstick of quality. Some people aren't used to an environment where excellence is expected."
>
> *Steve Jobs, Apple Computer co-founder and chief executive*

Your husband and boyfriend will see well-worn underwear. I had to laugh at Bridget Jones with her big knickers! How can you feel good about yourself when you are wearing tatty bras and knickers? Ask yourself when you check your underwear . . . if you were on a FIRST date would you wear that underwear? If the answer is no – then it is time to bag it for the charity shop or bin it.

If newly weds chop their hair short within one year of being married, how many of you used to dress up to meet your boyfriend to go to the movies and now don't?

Grooming is all about feeling your best and keeping your standards high.

I have an array of pretty silk nighties and baby dolls with matching housecoats. I love lovely underwear and beautiful night attire. It looks and feels luxurious and sexy. I wear it for myself to feel good, even when I don't have a boyfriend.

I was surprised however to hear from the guys in my survey for *Sexy Single and Ready to Mingle* book how many men liked lovely underwear and nighties on women and how many women didn't bother wearing it.

Beautiful underwear is a must, but even more important is a great fit.

Bras

Small or large boobs are both beautiful.

Good fitting bras are a must especially for the big-busted people. It is a shame when many naturally busted ladies, who haven't paid for them, actually try to hide them! So silly, when there are hundreds of women paying to get enlargements. Big boobs are beautiful – so if you have them be proud. Your boobs are an asset if the right fitting bra is worn. Hidden, they can change your posture and hurt your back. These are just two effects that big boobs have on the body, which small boobed babes don't even think about. Big boob also make you look as if you have a small waist. If not exercised, boobs can droop and make a girl look like they are hanging down onto her waist – not a good look if you want to look as if you have a waist!

When I say 'exercise' I don't mean bounce around – jogging can tear the muscle tissue and it makes the boobs droop further. I mean stretching and arm raises above the head and stretches for the pectoral muscles.

Bras now come in all shapes and sizes. Half-cup bras are very sexy and can be worn with dresses that are low cut to show off the cleavage. However these bras are not so great with T-shirts or fitted tops that can show the spill over and give you lumps that are not flattering. A full bra is better for this – One that has great support so that the bust stays high and out for a great silouette and frontal look.

Small boobs are beautiful too. For one thing you can go without wearing a bra and wear strapy dresses and T-shirts. As a smaller breasted person you can also wear padded bras and look fuller and gain that sexy cleavage without it being too much. These bras also give fullness for tight fitting tops and dresses that need more padding to give emphasis to the hour-glass look and a smaller waist.

Matching Bras and Nickers

We are all firstly attracted to the colour, style and fabrics. When buying underwear it is first most important to select the right bra that will fit – there are many underwear shops that sell lovely looking underwear on the rack, but when you put it on, you are squashed and squished with lumps and bumps and it really loses it's effect.

Makes sure it is the right fit and then I suggest you always buy in each particular design:

I x Bra

3 x bikini nickers

2 x larger nickers

3 x G-Strings

This way you have the whole set to suit different clothes. I always buy the G-strings a size bigger for comfort.

The bikini nickers can be worn with looser dresses.

The larger nickers for tighter skirts and dresses, where you don't want lines.

If they are really clingy I wear a G-String.

G-strings for trousers and shorts so that there are no nicker-lines.

Good fitting underwear is sexy. The colours ideally should tone with the clothes you are wearing. I like my shoes buy at the sale time and pick a new colour and style for that season to go with some of the coloured outfits that I have chosen to pick for that time.

The basic set colours are:

Black, navy, cream and white.

The black and navy always seem to keep their colour, but the cream and white definitely start looking grubby after a while. I chose to dye my beautiful cream underwear that have lost their crispness in the washing machine. Some underwear materials take the colour really well. I now have beautiful turquoises, lime greens, pale pinks…others are a disaster so I bin those.

You can build up your range because you can only wear one at a time so like the shoes they get less worn the more choices you have.

The more you spend on your underwear, often the more the design, colour, fit last and last and you definitely feel special. Some of the big clothing outlets however, are copying the designer stuff and the quality for the price is fantastic. You just have to shop around. My favourite designs are Aubard, Lejaby and la Perla. We have a lingerie shop opposite one of the Forever Young Clinics in Double Bay Sydney. Sylvia the owner stocks some amazing underwear and 'outfits,' nighties and swimwear. What surprised my staff and I more, was that her biggest client base are men. Yes men! They are buying this beautiful apparel for their ladies. How cool is that?

Now if you have a man in your life doing this well done. If you have a man, but he isn't train him…but make sure he knows your size and colour or send him to a shop that knows what you are wanting!

If it's down to you then start practising purchasing for yourself and the man you attract will most likely enjoy the beautiful underwear and nighties and know they bring you pleasure so that it will become second nature to him to buy you some for your birthday, treats and special occasions! We can all live in hope!

Bedrooms

Let us all imagine taking off our dress – perhaps in the semi-darkness to hide the cellulite to reveal beautiful underwear! How sexy! To shower and then step in to a beautiful sexy nightdress before slipping into clean sheets on a bed that looks inviting, in a room that looks special. With luck your partner may have ravaged you twice – once before the shower and once afterwards if you are lucky. Even so, it is still great for the soul to be able to pamper your self and feel special as you dose off to sleep with thoughts of gratitude and appreciation.

Adair's one of Australia's growing franchises for bed linen have a 'Linen Lovers Club.' I had to smile when they asked me to join, whilst buying new bedding. Your bedroom is one of those places that you spend many hours being close to that special someone if you are lucky. You personally deserve to sleep in crisp lovely sheets. Isn't it therefore important that you do have lovely sheets on your bed? Isn't it important to have a little mystery when you wear lovely night attire – even if it is flung off in the heat of passion?

Married people complain their sex life has become boring! Check out their bedrooms, their sheets and their night attire? I bet they are boring too!

To add some sizzle back into your life buy yourself new underwear and a fancy nightie you really like. Check your sheets on the bed and see if they need changing and keep your bedroom fresh.

Fashion

There's a brand new dance & I don't know its name,
Doo whap
Fashion.

We are the Goon Squad
& We're coming to town
Beep beep
Beep beep

Listen to me,
Don't listen to me,
Talk to me
Don't talk to me
Dance with me
Don't dance with me,
Don't
Beep beep

David Bowie

Chapter 9

Casual to Cocktail

⚐ TIP

Confidence is key to Couture.

SHELLEY SYKES
THE HAPPINESS GURU

Confidence is certainly key to couture or any form of dressing to impress. No matter how beautiful an outfit can be if the person wearing it is 'uncomfortable' or lacking confidence then their whole body language will portray this by cowering, looking down, pulling at the material, crossing their hands in front of themselves. Awkwardness ensues and as we have said several times 93% of communication is none verbal – we receive these messages of awkwardness and insecurity. The massage of love, beauty and confidence is lost. Yet on another person this same out fit with a confident demeanour will radiate.

Models really have 'to appear' confident walking down a catwalk otherwise they would never sell any outfits!

I say 'appear to be confident,' because many models have low self-esteem believe it or not. They feel the fear of what they do and do it anyway. They get their significance by being models and adoration from their audiences. Yet they are continually fighting an inner battle of self worth or being enough.

I have to admire them, because like leaders they take the challenge.

Like you, even though you may not feel confident at first; do as a model does – walk tall and put your arms by your side and smile, taking your first step and moving briskly with an air of 'knowing where you are going.' In an instant it changes your physiology. You become the confident person you 'look like.'

Now that you have the confidence sussed and model walk in the bag, it's time to know what to wear.

One simple dress can be classified as a day dress DEPENDING ON THE ACCESSORIES or cocktail dress.

Imagine a plain red dress, long sleeves or short sleeves it doesn't matter. Have a medium leather bag and matching red leather court shoes and a small gold necklace chain. Red lipstick. You can go to the shops, to work, lunch or visit the relatives. Yet look stunning in a casual way.

Wear the same red dress, but this time have a sequined small clutch bag, strapy sequinned shoes, darker eyeliner and still red lipstick, pearls or a bigger gold necklace and earrings and you are ready for after dinner drinks, cocktail party or dinner with friends.

This is just one example of how you can convert what you have to be appropriate giving you two amazing looks. The first is great for casual day and the night well it looks a much more expensive dress, because of the accessories and the way it has been styled.

You can do the same thing with jeans. Jeans and a 'Sexy Single' or 'Happiness T shirt' looks trendy and cool, appropriate for day wear – yet wear the same jeans with a shear blouse with sequins makes the outfit more glamorous for evening.

Casual or cocktail can be so close and yet are so different.

When an invite states '**Dress: Cocktail**' these are the options:

Cocktail for women:

- Short evening dress or $^1/_2$ length dress
- Classical glamorous look
- Feminine evening trouser suit.

Cocktail for men:

- Suit and tie.
- Jacket or Blazer with smart shirt & pants.

Dinner Dance or Ball Attire:

Dinner Suits for men:

- Tuxedo with bow tie & Cummerbund or waistcoat.

Women's options are:

- It can be a long glamorous dress, cocktail dress yet not normally trouser suit.

A ladies cocktail dress or outfit can be so exciting and interesting because of the different fabrics used.

Crepe – Some crepes can crease, but the Crepe de Sheen is shiny and light and crease proof. When cut on the bias it is beautifully boyant and drapes into folds.

Organza – is gorgeous over sold coloured lining materials, looking like a gossamer. It's shear and it can have a delicate pattern over a plan coloured fabric creating depth and luxury. You can also have evening jackets made from this material – see-through showing the outfit underneath yet glamorous and conventional covering the shoulders and another feminine layer that can be removed.

Silk – I love silk, because it can be shiny–silk satin and it looks very luxurious and smooth or it can be woven silk with threads of other colours shot through it giving it a sheen and depth or it can be matt and soft. What ever the choice, I always think silk defines luxury and glamour. The colour options are fantastic and suit all tones.

Chiffon – Is very elegant and feminine. All the old movie stars had chiffon scarves, chiffon dresses with long trains because this material is so plyable and can drape beautifully. Brilliant for all figure shapes when it is lined and the dress has benn made to fit properly.

Sequins – I love sequins and beads. They always look sparkly and glamorous. For the shy they may feel too noticeable but gee we are here on earth to shine and sequins definitely do under twinkling lights in a nightclub, cocktail bar at a dinner dance. They are an absolute pain to sew on yet in asia they specialise in this type of design and I always appreciate the art and hours that have gone into making such an outfit.

Even kaftans these days have sequins that make a plan top and trouser come to life.

Modern day Fibres – Are a superb accessory to the natural fibres such as lycra. This materia gives a shine and a fit to clothing and pings back in to shape at every wash! No ironing or very little is needed and that is great in my book – especially when you want your clothes to look as great after travelling to the other side of the world for a trip.

I would say that your choice of materials and style are definitely the key to the your success in the Cocktail Outfit Department.

Have fun shopping in the designer boutiques or try the big designer stores first and see what they suggest are the 'Cocktail' type outfits. Try them on and see which ones seem to fit and flow best to suit your personality, colour and body shape.

If you don't see one or can't find one that fits – buy the material and have one made. I looked everywhere for a Red satin long slinky evening dress for the Sexy Single Book launch Cocktail party. They just weren't in the shops at this time – I spent a day with my mum skimming through old copies of Vogue and Hello Magazines looking at the stars and their outfits and came across a design that I knew was perfect. It was made of red crepe satin. I cut out the design – a Valentino – Absolutely gorgeously feminine – he is one of my personal favourite designers. My dressmaker made up the dress to suit my body shape and we made a few changes to the design to be suitable for a cocktail event.

It was and still is one of my favourite outfits. I wore it with sequined red high heeled mules and matching sequined red clutch bag, red lipstick and my hair up in a French pleat to add to the sophisticated, elegant look. Anything is possible.

Everyone needs **at least one** beautiful cocktail outfit. Mostly they never date and you can build up from there.

Remember this is the time when the glamorous heels and handbag need to have as much care as the dress.

Make-up and hair should also be of a more evening, glamorous full style.

As mentioned this is where the family fur can be brought out, the Pashmina (as long as it tones in colour) or the little organza jacket or sequined bolero can be worn on the way to the event.

You never see the Film Stars walking the red carpet with a big duffle coat over their dresses or suit! So neither should you.

Cocktails are fun and flighty, sexy and sophisticated.

Enjoy!

Chapter 10

Beach & Boating

From early times we humans have lived by the sea, lakes and rivers. Initially for survival and ease of finding or growing food, transport and bathing. Now we still have that love of the water in our DNA, but most of us 'play' on the water with surfboards, boats, skis or jet skis...

We somehow feel re-energised when we are on or by the water.

Real estate is the most expensive on the coastline, because it is the most desired. I certainly love living near water and would ideally like my trendy office/TV studios to be situated on a jetty surrounded by water and then have a beachfront property for my home base. (One day that will happen! What we dream, we can achieve!)

Since many of us holiday near and around water or are lucky enough to live close by – our water living has definitely had and has an effect on our styling.

There is nothing nicer than seeing tanned healthy bodies carrying surf boards up an down the beach, whilst one lays on the beach and enjoy the rays of the sun.

There are some rules and only the few know.

Surfers have a particular fashion style to themselves. Trendy long bright board shorts that dry quickly so they don't get cold. Often matching the colours of their stylised Surfboards that have wild and wonderful colours, signatures or pictures of dolphins, girls or waves. The boards being a fashion statement and accessory – you could say an extension of their style and image.

They tend to like the body hugging slick-muscle defining board shirts that stop sunburn, if they are not wearing their cropped off at-the-knee wetsuits. Wild hair is the norm and for the girls it tends to be the same although most of the girls are longhaired Barbies on boards – these girls have a power and strength respected by the watchers and their fellow surfers.

Shoes that are 'in' these days seem to be the bright coloured 'Crocs' – rubber clogs that are so comfortable, sailors and yacht hands started to wear them out socially and now they are a 'fashion item.' They are fast replacing the expensive leather loafers.

Sailor gear is not cheap. Made for the wealthy jet set – shirts and shorts are all colour coordinated and have a certain designer look and feel.

Replicas are often great, because you can get a wardrobe of mix and match outfits sometimes for the price of one shirt and a pair of shorts.

Saying that, the quality is always wonderful.

There is nothing smarter and crisper than the whites, navy and reds, stipes or bold – to me it always has freshness to the boating look.

For women, very short skirts can mix and match with shorts and bikinis, dresses or three quarter length trousers.

I know many many women who refuse to wear swimwear by the pool or at the beach because they think they are 'too fat' or have unsightly stretch marks or legs or something. It is such a shame, because they are denying their bodies the rays of healing healthy sunshine. Remember brown fat looks slimmer than white!

At the end of the day if you are over weight you are over weight. You can commit to losing it by exercising more and eating less, yet in those times of transition you really can enjoy yourself. Everyone can see you are overweight with or without your clothes it just is. You can however wear a beautiful swim suit that is well fitted and the proper size and have a matching sarong and hat and look equally as fabulous as a thin, a old, or a young person. You stay cooler too. Big people tend to sweat more because the body is doing it's best to stay cool. This way you are doing your body a favour.

You don't have to parade up and down, just slip off your sarong and matching mules and lay and enjoy the peace and sunshine. When you need a swim walk to the edge and slip into the water. It is as simple and as elegant as that.

If you are really white, liquid tan solution gives you that extra colour, but you must remember to put on your sun block so you don't burn.

I personally believe it looks best when you have had a professional apply your tan evenly. You can then top up the colour yourself throughout the summer months if need be.

This is also great for those of you who are conscious about ankles or thicker legs – a little colour helps to give the appearance of slimness.

The secret is pretend to be confident. No body really cares what shape you are if they know you are lovely and having fun. Your outfits will detract from the parts you want to hide. Once again if you have a matching swimsuit, nail polished nails, beautiful sunglasses, towel and matching sarong you are still going to look glamorous!

Shine and enjoy sunny days by the water and live in appreciation. At the beach and in summer climates we often eat less and exercise more, so that can be an incentive too. Walking on the beach is as great as swimming. Remember to protect yourself though if you are out.

Matching caps and sunglasses are always a must especially if you are out in the sun.

Sunglasses are a style fashion accessory in their own right. From $10 to $1,000 there are plenty of options and it really does depend on your budget, size of face and preference. You can never get bored with sunglasses – especially if you are like me, one pair for every outfit and having a habit of leaving them all over.

Once in Cape Town I was walking down George Street and quite a few gorgeous men smiled and even girls stared as they walked past me. I felt great, thinking I must have been looking good – until I saw my reflexion in the window of one of the big department stores – I was wearing 4 pairs of sunglasses, 3 on my head, like hair bands and one pair propped on my nose. I laughed so much – remembering that morning that I didn't know where my sunglasses were... obviously three times!

Many mariners are filled with divine cruisers fitted out like floating designer homes. I love the movie with Goldie Horn who plays a Rich bitch and Kurt Russel a joiner. He is hired to fit out her cruiser with wardrobes and shoe holders made from the finest woods... Bring it on!

Style and glamour is still worn, whilst on the water or at the beach. Bikinis that are so miniscule with matching sarongs, with plenty of diamonds and bling bling. High kitten heels and a plethora of lipstick, mascara and moisture spray!

I do however believe wearing lots of jewellery at the beach is not so cool... it gets hot and burns the skin or leave marks.

Jewellery looks far better later in the day when you can show of your tan against the clean grease free pieces that glint and add a glow to your darkened skin.

Sarongs are one of the best most comfortable often colourful and crease free items of clothing ever invented for the beach or boat. I love these flimsy rectangular pieces of material because they can transform from a sexy skirt to a dress and hides the hips and bum for those shy of their bumps and lumps.

High or flat sandals are both cool. Some of the summer wedge heels thin the ankles and look sexy and are easy to walk in.

Beach bags and towels really should match. I even have a suntan cream bag inside the beach bag that matches each of my beach bags, which has it's own supply of creams so that I don't have to keep remembering to add creams to my bags or do a swap. It's logical and practical since I use all the bags a lot depending on the colour of the outfit, bikini and thus the colour of the towel and bag.

I just choose the colour of my bikini and then pick up the appropriate bag already packed with creams and towels. How easy is that?!

What to pack for a Beach or Cruise Holiday

For my holiday Cruise say for 7 days I would travel in:

- Beautiful silk trouser suit with camisole on flight or on ship
- Bra and matching G-string
- High-heeled shoes
- Sunglasses
- Handbag and Belt matching footwear.

Packed in my matching clean suitcase:

- Nightie and matching gown
- Travel silk kitten heel slippers
- I x bra and 7 x G-strings
- 2 x bikini nickers

Beach and Pool Attire

- 3 x Bikini or Swimsuits,
- 3 x Sarongs
- 1 x Towel
- Matching slip on footwear
- Beach bag and sun hat

Gym

- 3 x Gym shorts and tops
- 1 x Swimsuit
- 1 x pair of trainers

Day Attire

- 3 x Sundresses
- Matching hats
- Matching sunglasses
- 3 x shorts
- 3 x tops co-ordinated with bikinis
- 3 x matching slip on sandals – less if you can get away with co-ordination

Evening

- 5 x Cocktails dresses
- 1 x fancy top that can be removed and underneath have a sparkling top
- 1 x Sparkling bustier top
- 1 x long evening skirt
- 2 x long evening dresses with shoes to match and stockings
- Matching evening shoes to dresses and bags

Toiletries and Make-up

The best thing about cruises that you see so many different places and yet you have your suitcases unpacked and clothes hanging in the same spot for the duration.

On a cruise you also get to wear all your favourite clothes sometimes all in the one day!

Chapter 11

Pub or Party?

Many people may not make an effort to dress up to go to the pub, yet they would, to go to a party. I however, believe that if one makes an effort when dressing to go to the pub as if going to a party, you will more likely end up going to one – a party that is!

Pubs and parties aren't about drinking. They are about connecting with other people. New connections are made and friendships or acquaintances are developed. Therefore it is important to look ones best in a social place. Pubs really are an 'open to everyone party venue' if you think about it.

So how do you dress for the pub or a party? In Sydney there seems to be a party going on every day of the week. My photographic friend Bill, who works for the national newspapers and magazines, has about 60 functions a week to visit and photograph, from breakfasts to launch parties...

The delightful thing is that you can look as appetising at a breakfast morning meeting as you do at a fashion launch party that night. With a few changes to your accessories the change can be substantial. For a man a crisp suit and beautiful tie can transform into an elegant, but slightly more casual attire if the tie is removed and the shirt is of a quality that looks great with or without a tie and the shoes are clean and trendy.

Women can just touch up their make-up & add a little more jewellery & an extra spray of perfume even change their shoes to sandals & their handbag. It's that simple. Being prepared is worth feeling appropriate, gorgeous and comfortable.

With so many beautiful ties for men to choose from and coloured shirts men have so much more choice than they used to. Many men I know are starting to wear beautiful suits that may have only been worn for Sunday best or weddings now for work, so that they look just as good and just as glamorous. Grooming is all part of the communication that these guys are capable of managing themselves and therefore capable of looking after business – rightly or wrongly this is the visual communication.

In the city many men and women slip to the pub and wine bars after work to socialise and connect and so are still in their work attire. They are smart, looking powerful and women with the make-up get to be appreciated even more. The men in the suits attract more of the women. It's still 'the most successful' attracts 'the most beautiful'...the law of the jungle. It is important therefore to be congruent and as attractive in appearance at work, pub or party situation.

Sexy Singles could meet their soul mate at the pub after work.

In a country environment it is different again. Pub is an after dinner activity or a place to dine out. Changing from work attire to go to the pub is often a necessity. The change is uplifting and increases the confidence.

Change into what, you may say? Well a man may change into a beautiful shirt and smart jeans and jacket if he was meeting a lady, and the lady may also wear smart jeans, but with a feminine top or a sexy top and skirt.

There are exceptions to any rules...one place in Sydney by the harbour has an upstairs and also down stairs division. Upstairs all the well-dressed stylish looking people congregate to socialize. Downstairs guys turn up in shorts and flip flops or thongs...they tend to be rowdier and drink more than may be good for them. A blokey type of meeting place, where pubs are for drinking and recounting the sporting events of the week. Spookily the sporting professionals are upstairs in suits surrounded by scantily clad girlies, whilst the guys below connected by their love of sport, drink to their heroes in drunken camaraderie and often go home alone too rowdy and boisterous to attract a 'Sheila.'

Anything goes these days. Sunday best is now worn 7 days a week.

Dress your best to feel your best and you'll attract confident high self-esteemed people into your life.

Last night I went to the premier showing of 'Pricilla' at the theatre, converted into a play from the Australian iconic movie 'Pricilla of the Desert.' Three Drag Queens in a show travelling from Sydney into the heartland of Australia to Alice Springs by Combie Bus was quite a feat and the theatre depiction awesome with a real bus on stage. Their costumes were fantastic, make-up immaculate and their shoes matched their hemlines no matter what glamorous colourful outfit and wig they wore. These three were taking style to the limits and looking great all the way!

If I could capture them in a bottle and post them to you I would. No matter where these three landed – Hicks Ville or the bush, they dressed with style and glamour to suit their individual personalities. Some people on their journey knocked them for it, but they stood their ground to be congruent and happy with themselves.

At the end of the show it was a dream of one of the three, to see the sunset fully dressed in all 'her' splendour and to sing with her friends by her side. They had the most fabulous evening gowns on with matching headdresses and were wearing their walking boots. They created their own beauty in a beautiful place and enjoyed the journey climbing the red Rock in their outfits with comfortable shoes. The local Aboriginal people would have been proud of their respect and attention to dress if they saw them.

Chapter 12

Skiing &
Sporting Trips

We have all seen James Bond 007 swoosh down the mountain on ski's, either being chased by some baddies on snowmobiles or chasing some beautifully clad sex kitten on skis. Or picture him at the Races in Dubai, smart suit and lady in stunning big hat and high heels, or what about at the Grand Prix?

At the motor races the drivers are in designer leathers, the investors in suits and the models, well they too are in designer cat suits with chests popping out of push-up bras. It's all about glamour, style and appropriateness.

Ok going to football wearing a scarf and pom-pom hat isn't cool, but the players are dressed in designer shorts and shirts, boots and ball, trendy haircuts and their cheer team well, if our a hot blooded man you would want to howl. Face painting is a form of make-up, communicating your

passionate support of your team and belonging. It is becoming popular with adults as well as with the kids.

Sports have always attracted a following and now it is a big business even in the fashion world. Sports clothing manufacturers have expanded into the normal day to day clothing arena supplying kids and adults with footwear and tracksuits, T shirts and shirts. Nike does an amazing job at attracting a following for their colourful stylish designs playing on the winning formulae of a winning image by association.

Skiing

Let's take skiing as a unique fashion statement. Skiing fashion does not just extend to the great ski suit, skis, ski boots and matching poles, gloves and designer headgear or earmuffs. No, there is the designer snow-boots, the designer warm underwear and tops, and then there is the gear one has to wear, when not on the slopes. The fashionable Mink coat, the designer jeans and a whole array of beautiful tops that must be worn to keep looking attractive and eye-catching at the après ski parties. Not to mention the designer bikinis when having a sauna or steam ... if bathers are allowed! Then there is the nightclub out fit that needs to be packed too. Dancing is all part of this highly energetic sport. You need to have stamina to ski by day and party by night ... gee I miss it. Must schedule a ski trip soon!

Ok I know I can't leave it at that, you really want to know what to pack!

What to pack for a skiing Trip

For my ski holiday say for 7 days I would travel in:

- Mink coat or big long warm winter coat
- Smart blouse and waistcoat with matching jacket
- Bra and matching G-string
- Smart Trousers and high-heeled shoes or boots.
- sunglasses
- Handbag and belt matching footwear.

Packed in my suitcase:

- Bikini or Swimsuit, Sarong
- Towel
- Silk (warmer) Nightie and matching gown
- Travel silk kitten heel slippers
- I x bra and 7 x G-strings
- 2 x bikini nickers

Slope Attire

- Ski suit
- Matching headband and gloves
- Goggles
- 7 x pairs of ski socks
- 7 x polos/tops and blouses
- 1 x long johns and vest

Après ski

- 3 x Jodhpur trousers that look great with my boots
- 3 x fancy tops that can be removed and underneath have a sparkling top
- 1 x Sparkling Basque top
- 1 x Shear blouse that looks feminine and sexy
- 1 x Cocktail dress (one never knows) with shoes to match & stockings

Skis and poles

Ski boots

Toiletries and make-up

As you can see I am now covered for all occasions.

On the slopers for lunch I can unzip my ski suit to the waist and look pretty and warm with different jumpers and blouses.

After skiing I can go for a hot spa and steam.

For dinner and Après ski I have my beautiful coat and warm boots with Jodhpur-type trousers that look trendy with beautiful evening tops that be peeled off down to disco dancing attire.

Plus if there is a special event, cocktail or dinner I have a cocktail dress that will look glamorous and feminine.

You can mix and match to suit your personality.

My ski suit is a shimmer pink so I have the matching lipstick and I tend to wear tops during the day that look great with this suit – cobalt blues, pinks, cream, tans etc.

Chapter 13

Race Days & Wedding Days

I just love dressing for the races and it's the same for weddings. The preparation starts weeks in advance. The excitement builds. You have to decide which outfit you want to wear and marry it up with a suitably fashionable hat, heels and handbag. Perhaps two options just in case of the weather! It's not easy choosing one outfit that fits your personality, seems flattering to the figure and communicates our status, never mind two!

It is a big expense to prepare for either occasion, yet thousands of people do, because they know that this is where many peers will see them. It's a time to shine.

For the **Sexy Singles** the races are one of the best sporting spots to attract a new mate. Forget the horses. They are just an excuse to Dress to impress and mix and mingle with the gentry and the professionals. The horses are what attract the rich and competitive.

The men wear their best suits looking successful and on some occasions such as Ascot top hat and tails, just like in the movie *My Fair Lady,* looking powerful. Thousands of Men in suits – Smelling good, looking crisp with beautiful shirts and colourful ties it's quite a magnet for the sexy single fillies!

Women flock like beautiful butterflies with hats, heels and handbags that accent their outfits.

In recent years the bigger the hat and the scantier the dress attracted more attention. Unfortunately some of the ladies seemed to lose the plot and began looking too tarty and less attractive to those men they were trying to tempt or if the weather changed looked foolishly cold and in appropriately dressed.

The secret to dressing for the races is to look as glamorous and as vibrant as possible keeping sexy enough yet with decorum that would be acceptable in a modern day church.

What do I mean?

Well, dressing for the races or for a wedding, both very happy joyous expectant occasions, one needs to dress with style and sophistication.

It's about elegance both for the man and the woman.

Dressing for both the races and a wedding is an art.

Both occasions are a pinnacle of your wardrobe piste de resistance! Your best – a summation of the best you, your personality, what you are about and your standards.

I have been fortunate to have been picked as best dressed at the races on a couple of occasions, without even entering a fashion show.

Dressing well does not depend on age or size. It is about having the skill to pull everything together from your **Hat to Heels.**

WHERE DO YOU BEGIN?

It starts with the hat! Yes the hat. Hats that you really, really like are harder to come by than the little dress or suit that you can wear with it! I suggest you go looking and trying on. The trying is quite important because of your head and face shape, your height and your colouring.

For the mother of the bride this is so important. Mothers tend to decide on a colour and then buy an outfit and panic about finding a hat to match. Often ending up buying a hat for its colour and not it's suitability to the suit or dress, nor most importantly to their height and face shape.

Yes the hat is key and the first purchase. Depending on the hat colour, style and fabric then determines the type of outfit – suit or delicate feminine dress or trouser suit. The search begins yet if you find that there is nothing that you really like then there is always the dressmaker. I often have things made. They fit my body shape perfectly, the cut and colour are perfect and it is a designer one off outfit – very special.

For example, whilst in Paris, France I saw the most beautiful hat that was shaped like a flower petal. A purple cloche with pink and green petals flowing out of the brim. I had to try it on. It was a little big so they put a little nip into the band lining to make it perfect. It looked fab and suited my colouring as a spring tone and my face shape. I also have the personality and coincidence to wear it with joy. People stopped at the shop window, peering in, smiling and stuck their thumbs up as an approval sign, it looked good. The attendants were exuberant with the attention & gushed with compliments.

The important thing was that I felt good. I bought the hat and the box and brought it back to Australia. Spookily I had a beautiful Versace jacket with those colours. It was a great combination. Unfortunately though, the dress that went with the jacket was a little too heavy for the hat – the jacket was ok, but the dress needed to be more delicate if I was to wear the dress with the hat without the jacket.

Always remember to peel away like an onion so that each layer looks great in it's own right.

Many mothers of brides buy a suit and hat and when they co-ordinate their hats, heels and handbags they look fabulous. Yet once they get to the reception and take off their jackets and put down their handbags they are left with a camisole and skirt with shoes that may not be an exact match. They no longer look 'special.' As I have said you have to look fantastic as you peel away the layers.

Ladies do make sure that you buy a fabulous top that looks great with the skirt as a stand-alone outfit without the jacket. An option is to have a matching belt to the shoes and bag so that the shoes match and the outfit looks finished off or complete. Otherwise keep shopping until you get ALL the layers right.

I needed a plain pink or green dress made in silk georgette or something delicate. Despite my search I didn't find such a dress or skirt and top. Zilch! I did however find the perfect bag and strappy sandals. I was thrilled. I then made the decision to have a beautiful dress made in pink silk. Everything fit me perfectly and was totally colour co-ordinated. If the weather became cool I had my jacket, if it was hot I had a delicate dress totally colour co-ordinated with the hat, heels and handbag. It was a winning outfit.

My girl friends all loved the unusualness of the hat and the effect was soft and feminine, with enough cleavage to be flattering, which the men noticed of course!

Channel 7 TV were covering the Melbourne Cup, the most famous Australian Race Day and I was cornered to speak about my outfit, the style of the fashions that year and the races. As a professional speaker and experienced in TV, it was easy and a pleasure. My passion for fashion shone through.

One hour later I got a call on my mobile from my son, who excitedly told me I was on the news being interviewed every hour as part of their racing commentary for that day. He said it was cool! A compliment from a teenager is a rare gift indeed!

Nelson Mandela says 'who are we not to shine our light?'

Be your best and shine your light as often as you can. It's good for your heart and soul and everyone else's too!

Secret to dressing for the Races or a wedding in a nutshell:

TIP

The biggest secret to dressing for a wedding or the races is think 'Cocktail Glamour' with a Hat.

SHELLEY SYKES

The dresses of cocktail dresses are made from luxurious materials. They tend to be short to the knee or ballerina length. Fancy trouser suits are now acceptable, but the feminine dress is still the favourite.

Go for accessories that suit the season.

So if it is winter, you can go for a silk cocktail dress, but you may have a fur stole and hat with fur trimmings, stockings and court shoes rather than peep toe sandals – just as an example.

If it is summer you may go for a light big hat with a fine Pashmina or summery jacket and delicate bag and sandals as your accessories.

The colours should always be picked from your pallet. Light colours look great in winter as well as in summer. I have some beautiful cream wool winter suits as well as cream summer dress suits. The colour is always your choice. It's the fabric or accessories that depict the season.

Your smile and confidence wearing your chosen outfit makes you a winner every time!

WHERE TO SHOP

Well as I have said before shopping can be a chore or a delight.

Now that you know your body shape, your style, your colour pallet and your personality type that best suits your lifestyle shopping is going to be so much easier.

The first and easiest places to shop are some of the big department stores that have shops and designer brands all under the one roof.

You can start off in the hat department. Trying on hats is so much fun. Learning how to wear the hat is key and the shop attendants will help you there.

Knowing your face shape you have an idea now on the style that will best suit your face shape and height.

The next is to only look at hats that have those criteria and then fall in love with a hat that suits those dimensions and the colour that fits within your pallet. If you haven't found one that doesn't do it for you – DON'T BUY. There are other hat shops and stores. Try a few.

I sometimes fall in love with a hat and then find that it is double the price I was considering! I try it on one more time and then walk away to consider. I nearly always find a hat very similar after that and it usually is a third of the price and so I feel even luckier! I'm winning already! If it is still the hat I prefer than I will no doubt go back and make the purchase. You only live once and it makes an outfit it will be worth it's weight in gold.

Once you have your chosen hat – you take it will you, in it's hat box to the dress departments of the store. Usually go to the cocktail sections and look at the outfits there. Show the dress attendants your hat – they love to help and they love people who are on a mission. They know their stock inside out usually, unless they are casual staff. They will lead you to a rack with clothes that have the right colour or texture and it could be perfect.

If not don't buy move to the next section. Remember in the dress department you are now looking for a colour match in a style that suits your body in a fabric that you love and a style that you would gladly wear on your next holiday or cocktail party!

Keep making the rounds until you find the right outfit – otherwise find a style you love and get the material and have an outfit made to match your hat.

Once you have the material or dress go to the shoe department. The sandals or shoes have to fit and be the same tone as the hemline of the outfit preferably so when not wearing the hat they match the dress. If the hat tones then the hat, shoes and handbag must match.

DO NOT BUY a pair of shoes that match in colour but you personally don't like the style. The style is as important as the colour. You have to have them both right otherwise don't buy. There are the perfect bag and heels out there for you in your size! Just trust.

If you find the perfect pair of shoes but they don't carry the bag. Buy the shoes and continue on your search.

It is so exciting when your treasure hunt comes together and piece by piece they become the perfect winning outfit for you.

Putting all the items together you will know what type of underwear to wear. Just make sure it fits and feels fabulous.

Voila you are ready for the big day – Almost.

I recommend that everyone goes to the department stores once a year and has a professional make-up done just to stay modern and to watch and learn. See how they apply the make-up and take your hat so that they can choose colours that you will need to wear on the day. I suggest that people have an evening out wearing this make-up and see if they get compliments. If it works for you – you now know what to do on the special day for yourself or who to book for the make-up!

Now you are ready from **Hats to Heels**!

Vogue

Strike a pose
Strike a pose
Vogue, vogue, vogue
Vogue, vogue, vogue

Look around everywhere you turn is heartache
It's everywhere that you go [look around]
You try everything you can to escape
The pain of life that you know [life that you know]

When all else fails and you long to be
Something better than you are today
I know a place where you can get away
It's called a dance floor, and here's what it's for, so

Chorus:

Come on, vogue
Let your body move to the music [move to the music]
Hey, hey, hey
Come on, vogue
Let your body go with the flow [go with the flow]
You know you can do it

Chapter 14

Jewellery & Adornments

JEWELLERY

Just as with lines in clothes, choose your jewelry to emphasize your positive points and to draw attention away from your not so good ones. Buy carefully, so that you can mix and match different pieces just as with clothes.

Gold and pearl earrings, necklaces and pins, for example, are very versatile and can give you many different looks. You can wear them on their own, or mix and match them. A gold and silver chain and pearl necklace for instance, can be worn singly, or together, or even entwined together for an after-six look. It is very useful to collect pieces, which will play double roles. You really must like all your pieces. Earrings can double up as pins. Your jewellery can be a conversation piece and magnetize people to you. Always use your pieces of jewelry to attract attention.

You could wear your jeweler on your lapel or on a scarf draped round your shoulders. Always make sure any points are facing away from your figure faults or down if you have wide shoulders, up if you have a thick waist. If you have a small waist or hips, wear two earrings side by side there, or on a scarf you have draped around your waist.

Last year's hat can be made to look interesting and new with earrings clipped on the hatband, as can your shirt cuffs.

Choose the correct length of necklaces or chains to match your figure image: shorter if you have a long neck, longer if you have a short neck. If you have a large bust with a short neck, wear your necklace half way between your collarbone and bust.

EARRINGS

Earrings (which make everyone look "dressed") need to be considered very carefully as they are worn so near to the face. They should continue the line of the face or flatter it. Not many of us can get away with long dangly earrings, but remember for those who can, that they are not all that suitable for everyday or business wear anyway. Keep them for evenings.

ROUND SHAPED FACE: Choose earrings, which give a lift to the face, such as ovals or swirls, which are longer than they are wide. Teardrops are flattering, but long earrings, which dangle and end near the jaw line, are not good as they shorten and widen the face – more suitable to LONG NARROW FACES.

Other Accessories

Boats, Cars, Surfboards, Bikes, even Pooches in Pouches...

A boat, surfboard or even your car can be classified as an adornment.

Don't you remember your first car? I do. It was my pride and joy. I cleaned it all the time and gave it a polish even though it was an old model and second hand. When I managed to upgrade it to a sports car – well it was my baby! I had beautiful clothes, lovely jewellery and a car that was too small to fit a suitcase inside. My designer clothes had to be folded into a dustbin liner so that it could be moulded into the space to fit inside the car. My family thought I was mad buying a car instead of a house. Financially it probably wasn't wise but this car made me feel happy driving it and I had wheels to travel and see all my friends. It was also an outward extension of my style and personality. An accessory.

We see young men doing the same thing with their cars...painting them with amazing graphics, zooting them up and fitting them out with ear-bursting beat boxing hi-fi's. The surfers are as fond of their surfboards, waxing them lovingly and spraying them in designs that mirror their own style.

I remember from being 18 years young desiring a Porsche. I used to pretend that I was driving one until the day I did. What a great day. I still appreciate my car and I have had it about 14 years now.

Some men covert their golf clubs or their super stylish executive cars – to some they have these things and it means nothing. To others they are dreams come true and an extension of their personality. They bring joy and appreciation.

Some friends of mine have yachts. Their dream was to own a boat that they could entertain business colleagues in a wonderful environment and enjoy family trips out in style and glamour. Their boats are to some extent an accessory.

Just like me I fancy one day owning a helicopter so that I can jump in and beat the traffic and land on some beautiful penthouse roof and go for dinner or to a beach up the coast.

Anything is possible and we all chose accessories that suit our style, budget and lifestyle.

If you dream it you can achieve it.

Even families are an accessory…

My mother would say; I have my son Rory as a walking accessory, because I would co-ordinate his appearance with my own. Its fun! It's stylish and its congruent.

If you look immaculate and your car is filthy and unkempt it is not congruent. I like sleek clean desks, home with clutter free drawers and clean cars.

My friend Kurt likes dogs, horses, farms and kayaking.

Crista, likes glamour & style and has her favorite pooch in a designer pouch and takes her pet everywhere.

It's all about personal choice and preferences.

Chapter 15

Wardrobe &
Work Wear

TIP

Oh what to wear!
Pick appropriately and only buy clothes you like
and you will always look stunning!

SHELLEY SYKES
THE HAPPINESS GURU

As a stylist to the stars and many thousands of clients around the world for many years one of my jobs was to find clothes and styles that suited my clients:

- Lifestyle,
- Personality,
- Mood and
- The Occasion.

Each outfit had to fit into all 4 criteria's to be congruent with their persona that they were creating or had created. All the presidents and their wives have to become styled for their new roles as head of governments. Pop stars are continually reinventing themselves to match and mirror or reflect their new music. It's no good singing like Mary Poppins and dressing like a Hells Angel (although this Modern Day Mary Poppins sing-alike dresses like a pink rapper! – its true I have a rapping single!). Corporate businessmen dress differently to those working in a holiday resort for example.

WARDROBE PLANNER

PLANNING A SUCCESSFUL WARDROBE FOR YOU

- Choose clothes that are flattering to you and appropriate for your lifestyle.
- Choose clothes that emphasize your good body points and draw attention away from the parts of your body, which need camouflage.
- Styles must be appropriate for your career and life style and be able to mix and match.

Your existing wardrobe has to be taken into consideration

Look down your personal profile and mark off your: –

(a) Life style in order of priority (1) (2) (3)

   Career ( )   Social ( )   Casual ( )

(b) First and second colour characteristic

   (1) Tone _____   (2) Season _____

(c) Figure image _____   Scale _____

(d) Figure points to emphasize _____

   _____

(e) Figure points to camouflage _____

(f) List likes and dislikes _____

Now you are ready to plan a unique wardrobe for you.

This next section is fantastic. It takes time, but it will give you the tools to become more structured and organised with sorting out, which clothes can mix, stay, go or be a sensation as well as pointing out which clothes, hats or heels need to be added to complete a look.

First, start by planning a minimum basic working wardrobe that will take you through all the different situations you are likely to have to dress for during a week.

Plan on paper – I use a notebook, the three main colours or neutrals you are going to plan your wardrobe around. Now list jackets, skirts, trousers, blouses that you will need. Using your sketches as an outline, you add your preferences and your fashion tendency.

Remember, twelve carefully selected outfits will give you over forty different looks.

Now, only hang back into your wardrobe the clothes you have listed which will fit the bill and are in good condition. Next make a list of the gaps in your wardrobe (remember – in order or priority).

Do the same for your casual and social wardrobe.

When you go shopping, only buy garments, which are on your list.

Follow the same guidelines for your accessories.

Hats to Heels

ITEMS OF CLOTHING THAT I ALREADY HAVE

	DAY	EVENING FOR WORK	BOTH
BLOUSES	_____	_____	_____
CAMISOLE	_____	_____	_____
VEST	_____	_____	_____
SWEATER	_____	_____	_____
CARDIGAN	_____	_____	_____
T SHIRTS	_____	_____	_____
SWEAT SHIRT	_____	_____	_____
DRESSES	_____	_____	_____
SKIRT	_____	_____	_____
SHORTS	_____	_____	_____
TROUSERS	_____	_____	_____
JACKET	_____	_____	_____
WAISTCOAT	_____	_____	_____
TOP COAT	_____	_____	_____
RAINCOAT	_____	_____	_____

Notes:

_____

_____

FOR SOCIAL

BLOUSES _____ _____ _____

CAMISOLE _____ _____ _____

VEST _____ _____ _____

SWEATER _____ _____ _____

CARDIGAN _____ _____ _____

T SHIRTS _____ _____ _____

SWEAT SHIRT _____ _____ _____

DRESSES _____ _____ _____

SKIRT _____ _____ _____

SHORTS _____ _____ _____

TROUSERS _____ _____ _____

JACKET _____ _____ _____

WAISTCOAT _____ _____ _____

TOP COAT _____ _____ _____

RAINCOAT _____ _____ _____

Notes:

_____

_____

_____

_____

FOR CASUAL

BLOUSES   _____   _____   _____

CAMISOLE   _____   _____   _____

VEST   _____   _____   _____

SWEATER   _____   _____   _____

CARDIGAN   _____   _____   _____

T SHIRTS   _____   _____   _____

SWEAT SHIRT   _____   _____   _____

DRESSES   _____   _____   _____

SKIRT   _____   _____   _____

SHORTS   _____   _____   _____

TROUSERS   _____   _____   _____

JACKET   _____   _____   _____

WAISTCOAT   _____   _____   _____

TOP COAT   _____   _____   _____

RAINCOAT   _____   _____   _____

Notes:

_____

_____

_____

ITEMS OF CLOTHING THAT I NEED

	DAY	EVENING FOR WORK	BOTH
BLOUSES	_____	_____	_____
CAMISOLES	_____	_____	_____
VEST	_____	_____	_____
SWEATER	_____	_____	_____
CARDIGAN	_____	_____	_____
T SHIRTS	_____	_____	_____
SWEAT SHIRT	_____	_____	_____
DRESSES	_____	_____	_____
SKIRT	_____	_____	_____
SHORTS	_____	_____	_____
TROUSERS	_____	_____	_____
JACKET	_____	_____	_____
WAISTCOAT	_____	_____	_____
TOP COAT	_____	_____	_____
RAIN COAT	_____	_____	_____

Notes:

_____

_____

Hats to Heels

FOR SOCIAL

BLOUSES	_____	_____	_____
CAMISOLES	_____	_____	_____
VEST	_____	_____	_____
SWEATER	_____	_____	_____
CARDIGAN	_____	_____	_____
T SHIRTS	_____	_____	_____
SWEAT SHIRT	_____	_____	_____
DRESSES	_____	_____	_____
SKIRT	_____	_____	_____
SHORTS	_____	_____	_____
TROUSERS	_____	_____	_____
WAISTCOAT	_____	_____	_____
TOP COAT	_____	_____	_____
RAIN COAT	_____	_____	_____

Notes:

_____

_____

_____

_____

FOR CASUAL

BLOUSES _____ _____ _____

CAMISOLES _____ _____ _____

VEST _____ _____ _____

SWEATER _____ _____ _____

CARDIGAN _____ _____ _____

T SHIRTS _____ _____ _____

SWEAT SHIRT _____ _____ _____

DRESSES _____ _____ _____

SKIRT _____ _____ _____

SHORTS _____ _____ _____

TROUSERS _____ _____ _____

JACKET _____ _____ _____

WAISTCOAT _____ _____ _____

TOP COAT _____ _____ _____

RAINCOAT _____ _____ _____

Notes:

_____

_____

_____

 Hats to Heels

I HAVE THE FOLLOWING ACCESSOREIS

	DAY	EVENING FOR WORK	BOTH
HATS	_____	_____	_____
SCARVES	_____	_____	_____
EARRINGS	_____	_____	_____
NECKLACES	_____	_____	_____
BROOCHES	_____	_____	_____
BELTS	_____	_____	_____
HANDBAGS	_____	_____	_____
SHOES	_____	_____	_____
BOOTS	_____	_____	_____

Notes:

_____

_____

_____

_____

_____

_____

_____

FOR SOCIAL

HATS _____ _____ _____

SCARVES _____ _____ _____

EARRINGS _____ _____ _____

NECKLACES _____ _____ _____

BROOCHES _____ _____ _____

BELTS _____ _____ _____

HANDBAGS _____ _____ _____

SHOES _____ _____ _____

BOOTS _____ _____ _____

Notes:

FOR CASUAL

HATS   _____   _____   _____

SCARVES   _____   _____   _____

EARRINGS   _____   _____   _____

NECKLACES   _____   _____   _____

BROOCHES   _____   _____   _____

BELTS   _____   _____   _____

HANDBAGS   _____   _____   _____

SHOES   _____   _____   _____

BOOTS   _____   _____   _____

Notes:

_____

_____

_____

_____

_____

_____

_____

_____

_____

I NEED THE FOLLOWING ACCESSORIES

	DAY	EVENING FOR WORK	BOTH
HATS	_____	_____	_____
SCARVES	_____	_____	_____
EARRINGS	_____	_____	_____
NECKLACES	_____	_____	_____
BROOCHES	_____	_____	_____
BELTS	_____	_____	_____
HANDBAGS	_____	_____	_____
SHOES	_____	_____	_____
BOOTS	_____	_____	_____

Notes:

_____

_____

_____

_____

_____

_____

_____

FOR SOCIAL

HATS	_____	_____	_____
SCARVES	_____	_____	_____
EARRINGS	_____	_____	_____
NECKLACES	_____	_____	_____
BROOCHES	_____	_____	_____
BELTS	_____	_____	_____
HANDBAGS	_____	_____	_____
SHOES	_____	_____	_____
BOOTS	_____	_____	_____

Notes:

_____

_____

_____

_____

_____

_____

_____

_____

_____

FOR CASUAL

HATS   _____ _____ _____

SCARVES   _____ _____ _____

EARRINGS   _____ _____ _____

NECKLACES   _____ _____ _____

BROOCHES   _____ _____ _____

BELTS   _____ _____ _____

HANDBAGS   _____ _____ _____

SHOES   _____ _____ _____

BOOTS   _____ _____ _____

Notes:

_____

_____

_____

_____

_____

_____

_____

_____

THINGS TO REMEMBER

SCALE	FABRIC WEIGHT	DETAILS
TEXTURE	FABRIC TYPE	PRINTS
ACCESSORIES	DARTS	SEAMS
PLEATS	SLEEVES	LAPELS
COLLARS	POCKETS	JACKETS
NECKS		

LEVELS OF CONTRAST – COLOUR

BEST LEVEL OF CONTRAST FOR ME

- ASSERTIVE LOOK
- ROMANTIC LOOK
- GLAMOUR LOOK

With a wardrobe plan we can make headway understanding the loop hoes we have in our wardrobe. We don't have to fill all the missing holes in one go...we can work up to those items as and when we see the items we need or as when the event arises that will be perfect 'if only'…

Some of you high fliers will benefit from a complete wardrobe straight away and that can easily be fixed with a Personal Shopper and the list you have just come up with. It's as easy as that. Anything that they bring back for you that you don't like they can return.

It takes out some of the fun but it also takes out some of the chore of looking and searching for the items. Once you have a complete wardrobe life becomes so much simpler and easy to manage. Packing for business trips is no longer a burden and you can be colourful for once and have a wardrobe that suits you!

Working Wardrobe for Men

For example a successful business man that travels a lot with his work and is taken out for meals by clients, attends gala dinners, yet when at home goes sailing on his boat and enjoying relaxing and socializing with his social bubbly wife and their kids.

This man will have probably:

- Dinner suit and matching accessories with several cummerbunds
- 6 great suits varying in colours from Navy to Cream.
- 12 beautiful shirts from white to a variety of colours.
- Strong bright ties with some coloured shirts to match his suits and ties.
- 8 pairs of shoes, 3 pairs x black, brown, navy, cream, boating loafers, moccasins with matching belts.
- 3 x Sailor type sweater and matching shorts
- 3 x swimmer shorts and T shirts
- 4 pairs of casual smart tailored trousers
- 2 x pairs jeans
- 5 x stylish casual shirts
- 2 x silk knit fine jumpers
- 3 x stylish T shirts
- 3 x $1/2$ cropped casual trousers
- 1 x leather jacket
- 1 x casual cashmere jacket
- 1 x over coat long
- 1 x rain jacket short

This man will be fitted out now ready for any type of occasion that suits his life. The colour of ties and shirts show and

reflect his personality. The quality of cut of his suits defines this man with high self-esteem.

His foot-ware (and women check shoes guys) matches his different styles of clothing, whether smart or casual.

Even his casual is trendy, yet stylish.

The words here are 'appropriate'.

TIP

Ties are a way a man can set the mood of the meeting.
Gold for Leaders, *confident and calm.*
Red for Power and Achievement.
Blues – Negotiation.
Green for Great Integrity.
Pink for PR.

SHELLEY SYKES
THE HAPPINESS GURU

Working Wardrobe for Women

Business ladies are similar, but they can mix in their wardrobes dresses that are stylishly cut with colour for work that can be blended with jackets and mixed with colour and of course the selection of shoe styles, heights, colours can be far more varied. Women are lucky too that the selection of evening wear can be so glamorous yet come in different styles and lengths from long to cocktail, to clingy and short or evening trouser suits...

It always surprises me that in sunny cities like Sydney and Cape town at lunch time when the office workers leave their modern blocks for lunch it is a mass of black dressed bodies mixing and mingling. Almost like a uniform in these two beautiful cities the women workers are wearing black suits with frumpy white blouses, black court shoes and a big black bag. It's the same even in London and no doubt in New York.

Please take it from me YOU DON"T NEED TO WEAR BLACK TO BE TAKEN SERIOUSLY.

Let us blast away myths about BLACK.

Black does NOT make people look slimmer.

Cut and style do.

Black does not make you shine. Black actually makes you blend or become insignificant. If you want to disappear then wear black. Colour helps you shine.

Black does show up marks, dandruff and other spills sometimes mores so. So wear colour its more fun.

Black does not make you look more serious. Takes rather than gives. Employers want givers and go getters. Look like one and you will get promoted.

Black is only easy because you have the bag and shoes. Buy a suit and matching bag and shoes and that will be as easy. Try a whole new colour – red is great for power and energy. Wear red lipstick and make-up and you will be taken seriously.

I mention all this because for many years women have been working hard in the offices of the big cities and doing outstanding jobs competing with men in dark suits.

Ladies listen: **You don't have to compete by dressing like a man.** The way to win is by being the unique soulful colourful you. Most of the women leaders running empires and there are far more today than ever before are make-up wearing colourful beings! Emulate them and not the girls next to you!

A ladies working wardrobe depends on personality and type of work.

Uniforms are great because they are easy. Your wardrobe can be easy too. You don't have to have one wardrobe just for work and one for pleasure. You can mix and match. Ok you wouldn't go to work in a cocktail dress unless you were a hostess of some kind but you can wear your summer dress to work that you wear out on occasions.

Wardrobe for women

This woman will have probably:
- Smart coat dress and matching accessories
- 6 great suits varying in colours from Navy to Cream
- 12 beautiful blouses from white to a variety of colours
- 3 cocktail dresses
- 8 pairs of shoes, some with heels some flat
- 3 x Sailor type sweater and matching shorts
- 3 x swimsuit and sarongs
- 4 pairs of casual smart tailored trousers
- 2 x pairs jeans
- 5 x stylish casual tops
- 2 x sequined tops/day/night
- 3 x stylish T shirts
- 3 x $\frac{1}{2}$ cropped casual trousers
- 1 x leather jacket, can be in a colour
- 1 x casual cashmere jacket
- 1 x over coat long
- 1 x rain jacket short

Remember many people socialize and work far more than they do play at the weekends.

YOU MAY AS WELL LOOK YOUR BEST AT WORK AS YOU DO ANYWHERE.

When I worked at IBM in the corporate world I had several suits with beautiful flattering blouses all that I liked. Now suits are made in a variety of colours cuts and shapes to suit everyone.

As a speaker I am still expected to turn up looking smart and appropriate – yet I can still wear beautiful flowing dresses and colourful suits.

A mum with 2 kids can still have an exciting wardrobe. You don't have to have the token 'trakki' (tracksuit) with baggy bottom and bulging knees. Think 'Desperate House Wives' wardrobe. On that TV show the mums definitely look sexy, but are still practical at the appropriate times and all dress to suit their personalities...

... And this is what you need to do for yourselves too.

Chapter 16

Property Styling

🏃 TIP

Your home is a reflexion of your personality & Style.

**SHELLEY SYKES
THE HAPPINESS GURU**

Styling of your surroundings can add so much value to your life by making you **'feel great'**.

I have always maintained that your own home should reflect the **personalities and interests** of those living there and be **a place of inspiration** and **revitalization.**

It really doesn't matter if you own your home or rent it. You need to select the location and place that suits you. When I lived in Johannesburg, South Africa I moved into a large house with pool and tennis courts and shared the living expenses with 5 other business executives. We had a lifestyle that individually at that time none of us could afford separately, but collectively it was great.

I made my room an extension of my personality with bright pictures and beautiful bedding sets. When I moved to my own little cottage in Cape Town I was able to buy my first set of red pans and designed my dinning table and chairs to fit on the wall as art work when I didn't have guests. My bed was on stilts and my office underneath. It was perfect for my bright bubbly personality and I loved going home and inviting guests. With my pink car parked outside in my twenties I was congruent.

Some of you may think it is all about expense or things – it really isn't. It's about what makes you feel good. I still like IKEA stuff. It's bright colourful and quite cheap and I'm not a cheap chick by any means. I do like colour and I do like the modern style and Ikeas can provide good quality modern items that suit my personal needs. My family on the other hand love antiques and traditional pieces that hold their own beauty for them.

My pictures in my home and certain artefacts that I have picked up on my journeys around the globe are what give me the greatest joy as well as freshly cut Star Gazer lilies that fill the air. My picture from the Amazon brings a smile to my face when I walk into my apartment. I have two large green bronze stalks that are another holiday memento and silver disk plate with the brightest Brazilian Blue butterflies not forgetting the stuffed Piranha fish I caught one Christmas, in the bathroom.

The colours I have chosen for the lounge and dining room are cobalt blue and turquoise and the outside chairs are turquoise too. All my bedrooms are themed. We currently have my son's room 'Out of Africa', mine is Princess Shelley's with canopy and 2 massive mattresses so the bed is huge and high and our guest bedroom is 'Going Japanese.' All fun and fabulous! We love living her and friends love to visit.

I really suggest that you review each room of your house and see if you can remove clutter and highlight some article or piece that you really love. This piece can be the catalyst for your choice in colour of the room. For example I have two blue vases – I just love their colour – periwinkle blue. I used these vases as my focal point of the room, to match up the leather settees in the lounge and then the rug. It's sometimes as simple as that. Here are some more ideas.

HOME ENVIRONMENTS

When the proverb says **'Home is a person's castle'** it really means a place of:

- Protection
- Beauty
- Pride
- Entertainment and merriment
- Recharge or tranquility – a retreat
- Fair play
- Reflection
- Family and friends

Our home can be beautiful no matter what our financial state.

With beautiful surroundings by adding **colour** and **positive noises and smells it will** have an **emotional uplifting effect** on the entire household? This is why so many people are spending so much money on DIY and the renovation TV shows are so popular.

My TV show **Feng Shui** gave people ideas and tips on how to place colour and how to style their homes and gardens to suit their personalities...and not that of the stylist. It was a hit and perhaps a little before it's time.

Now TV shows are clambering for the ratings to help its eager audience...so producers if you need an expert out there give me a ring! I have the right formula to raise your ratings!

It is quite simple.

Add personal touches and surround yourself with your interests with colours you love.

From single studio apartments to mansion waterfront dream homes they can be made to look and feel like an extension of yourself and your own personal branding.

Professional Help

If you need:-

- Great ideas and help with adding your interests to your place
- A Style profile
- Help with a new pad make-over
- Help to change the old pad to reflect the new you
- De Cluttering **and Stylish presentation before a sale**

Check out **www.beautifulunlimited.com** Property Styling

We spend so much time at work we really need to return home to a pleasant experience...

Most people invest a large chunk of their earnings into their homes.

It might as well reflect, who you are and where you are going!

You Deserve it!

Indoor Accessories

Water features inside properties **sound, look** and **feel great.** The **Feng Shui** philosophies state that **water attracts wealth!** Your **personal identity** has to play a key role in your choice to keep integrity for the image and feel of your place. **Furniture** and **furnishings** should be a **reflection of your branding or personality** unless you are furnishing an investment property, even though it should still be a place that reflects your standards and the target market you aim to attract. Fresh flowers are a wonderful addition to a home or office. They smell great, look great and they are actually healthy for you, because they raise your body mega hertz keeping your energies high.

 TIP

A sniff of flowers a day, keeps the doctor away!

SHELLEY SYKES
THE HAPPINESS GURU

I love the smell of Oriental lilies, gardenias, jasmine and lavender. Investment property accessories – Neutral colours and simple lines are best.

Many people want their environments to reflect their status, lifestyles and personalities, but are not sure how to do it or don't have the vision.

TV programs have given the viewers the "look, learn and copy" ability to duplicate stylists that often would be too expensive for themselves to justify or afford.

The downfall of this approach is that often stylists have imprinted their own tastes and style without regard to their individual needs or lifestyles.

So where are we at?

Cooking, Lifestyle and DIY programs are still hugely popular with the highest ratings in the States, UK and here in Australia and still growing. The revenue for the TV stations is phenomenal and so now nearly every channel is trying to take a cut of this expanding market.

The viewers however are increasingly becoming more sophisticated and I believe wise to these tired and outdated approaches to house, garden and personal makeovers.

This is where I come in!

It has always been down to timing. The time is now calling for the "Holistic Approach" It has now grown from people wanting "off the shelf" type styling to a "personally designed bespoke" design tailored to an individual's needs.

Using birth charting with the accurate Chinese system of Feng Shui you can apply personal styling, colours, shape and texture analysis relevant to that persons personality and experiences. This can be extended into your home, office garden and environment. I believe this is the way forward. The feeling of wellness and balance with the environment is key to the holistic approach. Online advice, fact sheets, and video and book sales could support this concept.

Many presenters fail when they do not have the expertise or knowledge in the field they are representing. This is why programs such as "Ground Force" have proven to be so successful they use professionals. The Cooking programs use professional chefs.

So with the new holistic concepts it is imperative to use a professional beauty therapist, interior designer, a Feng Shui consultant and astrologist. This starts to become expensive unless one person has all these experiences! Is there such a person or company? Yes. **www.beautifulunlimited.com**

Look out for future shows or check www.shelleysykes.com and sign up for a free newsletter.

Shelley's ABC for Styling...

Always shine your shoes

Buy the best bra and bikinis to fit your bum and boobs

Clear your closet every now and then

Dress to Impress and still be you

Experiment with colour and combinations

Follow your own intuition

Get rid of cellulite with Forever Young's G5's

Have fun

Imagine and create your own look

Judge no one

Know what you want

Live in gratitude and laugh more

Measurements are better than scales

Never leave home without your lipstick

Opt for a smile

Passion is possible

Queens to the Quiet, can still shine their magnificence

Remember life is a journey you can be anything

Stay true to whom you are

Treat others with respect

Understand nothing is wrong. It just is

Visualize what you really want

Win – win there are no losers

X-ercise to keep firm

You are beautiful inside and out

Zz spend more time sleeping

Chapter 17

Hats to Heels Tips

TIP

Hats can Heighten and flatter the Eyes.
Tip your hat carefully.

SHELLEY SYKES
THE HAPPINESS GURU

TIP

The Higher the Heel,
the Thinner the Ankle looks.

SHELLEY SYKES
THE HAPPINESS GURU

TIP

Confidence carries the legs and
the gaze of others further.

SHELLEY SYKES
THE HAPPINESS GURU

TIP

Make-up makes a difference.
Wear it and earn 30% more than those that don't.

SHELLEY SYKES
THE HAPPINESS GURU

TIP

Faces need smiles.
Nails neat.
Shoes should shine.

SHELLEY SYKES
THE HAPPINESS GURU

TIP

Glowing skin gives a lift to any garment.

SHELLEY SYKES
THE HAPPINESS GURU

TIP

Every layer of clothing peeled off like an onionskin,
Should be as succulent as the next layer.

SHELLEY SYKES
THE HAPPINESS GURU

TIP

*The best universal accessory around the globe
is a SMILE.*

**SHELLEY SYKES
THE HAPPINESS GURU**

TIP

*Accessories suit your personality. Quietly confident people
look great in delicate simple real gold and platinum
with the shades of gems that suit their outfits.*

**SHELLEY SYKES
THE HAPPINESS GURU**

TIP

Matching underwear is a Must.

**SHELLEY SYKES
THE HAPPINESS GURU**

TIP

*Shoe colours should ideally tone with
The hemline of trousers or the skirt hemline.*

**SHELLEY SYKES
THE HAPPINESS GURU**

TIP

Cut and colour define the style of an outfit.
It's the person wearing it that brings an outfit to life.

SHELLEY SYKES
THE HAPPINESS GURU

TIP

Bags, Belts and Boots should all match.

SHELLEY SYKES
THE HAPPINESS GURU

TIP

When out shopping aim to buy clothes and accessories
that are on your shopping list and not by impulse
unless you really, really like it.
When you find something special that is always a great buy.

SHELLEY SYKES
THE HAPPINESS GURU

TIP

Hair cut, colour and condition can define
a person's personality.

SHELLEY SYKES
THE HAPPINESS GURU

TIP

*A person's smile is their invitation card
to most parties.*

**SHELLEY SYKES
THE HAPPINESS GURU**

TIP

Style is personal. Anything is possible.

**SHELLEY SYKES
THE HAPPINESS GURU**

TIP

*Always have one outfit that you really love with
matching shoes and bag that makes you feel fabulous in
good condition – ready to be worn in case of a surprise event.
Be prepared.*

**SHELLEY SYKES
THE HAPPINESS GURU**

TIP

*Belts, bags and shoes should match or at least tone in colour.
Make sure you love the design.*

**SHELLEY SYKES
THE HAPPINESS GURU**

 **TIP**

The best accessories I have ever had are a good looking,
stylish man on my one arm and diamonds on the other.

SHELLEY SYKES
THE HAPPINESS GURU

 **TIP**

Great grooming includes the respect of others
and their personal tastes.

SHELLEY SYKES
THE HAPPINESS GURU

 **TIP**

Good health harvests happy humans.
Stay fit and firm and you'll look good with or without
your clothes.

SHELLEY SYKES
THE HAPPINESS GURU

 **TIP**

Oral hygiene is a must for a beautiful smile
and great breath.
Brush regularly and ensure that you have a toothbrush
or floss with you for touch ups.

SHELLEY SYKES
THE HAPPINESS GURU

TIP

*Figure and fit are by far the best or worst asset
a woman can have.*

**SHELLEY SYKES
THE HAPPINESS GURU**

TIP

*If the Fit is great for the figure you can look fantastic.
Never go too tight. Even the skinniest look fat.*

**SHELLEY SYKES
THE HAPPINESS GURU**

TIP

*If you feel fake - Re-assess your outfit.
There will be something that is incongruent with your outfit.
Always trust your intuition.*

**SHELLEY SYKES
THE HAPPINESS GURU**

TIP

*Black is not always flattering. Make sure
that the outfit colour suits your skin type and gives you a
youthful energised glow. People that way will be
looking at your face that way and not your size.*

**SHELLEY SYKES
THE HAPPINESS GURU**

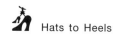

🎩 TIP

Colour combinations can be such fun. Play with the colours you have and see what colour is being classified as 'fashionable' and pick it out of your wardrobe and mix and match it with other colours to have a 'trendy' feel.

**SHELLEY SYKES
THE HAPPINESS GURU**

🎩 TIP

Stockings are sexy and the shiner they are the more luxurious – just make sure that they elongate your leg not fatten them.

**SHELLEY SYKES
THE HAPPINESS GURU**

🎩 TIP

Fabric textures frequently shape the designer and stimulate responses of look, touch and feel.

**SHELLEY SYKES
THE HAPPINESS GURU**

TIP

*Firm neckline and jaws can be achieved without surgery.
The modern hi-tech Forever Young equipment is
amazing for wrinkle reduction and muscle tightening.
Check it out before considering surgery or post surgery
to keep everything firm and full.*

**SHELLEY SYKES
THE HAPPINESS GURU**

TIP

*Height of heel depends on the suitability
and location of the outing.
Usually low heels for casual and higher
the more glamorous and elegant the occasion.*

**SHELLEY SYKES
THE HAPPINESS GURU**

TIP

Glamour and Grace are a Girls Gift to a Guy.

**SHELLEY SYKES
THE HAPPINESS GURU**

SHELLEY SYKES

THE HAPPINESS GURU

Hats to Heels

Learn how to Dress to Impress & Still be You

Your Appearance can help you achieve the desired goal **without even opening your mouth**

Learn how to:
Attract your Soul mate
Increase your Credibility
Look Sexily Attractive for your Age
Boost your Income
Make a Statement
Look Younger
Be Appropriate
Impress
Book Now

HAPPINESSGURU

Shelley Sykes

BSc MBA Dip Psych Dip Journo
PO Box 452, Concord 2137 NSW Sydney
P: +61 438 016 622   F: +61 2 8765 0270
e-mail: shelley@shelleysykes.com
www.shelleysykes.com

Hats to Heels
Style Seminars

Dress to impress and still be you

Sexy City Styling with Shelley Sykes.

Learn all the concepts that Shelley has shaired with you in this book. This is an opportunity to hear it 'from the horses mouth.'

See designer outfits. Learn how to dress to impress and still be you. Get the information you need to shine and live your best life.

Check out the events page on the website and see when the next style seminar is happening in your city and sign up for a free news letter.

www.shelleysykes.com

Beautiful Unlimited Personal Styling

Style Seminars to learn Styling Skills
Wardrobe sort with a stylist
Make-up lessons with make-up artist

Personal Consultations with Shelley Sykes

Learn to become an image consultant

How to series ... CD's $49.95

How to series... DVD 's $495.00
With Book

Personal Styling Service offers:

Personal Analysis and Colour Assessment
Wardrobe Sort
Shopping Service
Personality and Lifestyle Clothes Matching
Photographic documentation for ease of selection
Attendance at Fashion shows to help with selection
Physiology and Deportment Training

All the above or any combinations of the services are chargeable plus expenses.
International or National travel is a possibility.

Check www.beautifulunlimited.com or email: beautiful-ltd@bigpond.com

Book Shelley as a TV Presenter or Speaker
www.shelleysykes.com

Be Good Look Gorgeous

Head Office:

Rua Jose Getulio, 579 –Cj
111/112 – Liberdade
CEP 01509-001
Sao Paulo – SP
Telephone (+55 11)3341 6457

Offices in Brazil, USA, Australia, Canada, Japan, United
Kingdom and Scandinavia

www.bluebrazil.com.au
info@bluebrazil.com.au

www.bluebrazil.com.br
info@bluebrazil.com.br

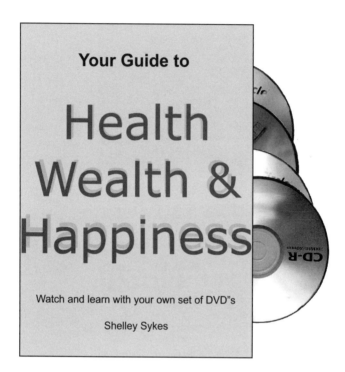

Your Guide to

Health
Wealth &
Happiness

Watch and learn with your own set of DVD"s

Shelley Sykes

$495.00

www.shelleysykes.com.au

Health, Wealth & Happiness DVD's

No time to re-read the book but want some revision?

What better way than to be entertained, whilst you learn from ordinary people doing extraordinary things and achieving impossibilities?

Watch and learn with your own set of DVD's...

 Dream and Achieve

 Style and Image

 Wealth Creation

 Goals and Beliefs

 Health and Happiness

5 DVD's with hours of interviews and hundreds of tips from Celebrities, Olympic Champions, Gurus such as Edward de Bono and Siimon Reynolds and many more inspirational people living their dream lives and teaching you the tips and tools to make it yourself.

Order it NOW from **www.shelleysykes.com**

All inclusive special deal for readers $495.00

Forever Young

Forever Young,
I want to be Forever Young
Do you really want to live forever,
forever and ever

Youth Group

Connect4Love

Expensive - Discrete – Personal – Successful – Match-Makers

Happiness is...a loving relationship

Shelley Sykes – The Happiness Guru

- **Are you a high flyer and too busy yet looking for love?**
  Connect4love can organise your dates between business trips!

- **Are you a CEO or Celebrity that need discretion?**
  Connect4love is totally private and personal

- **What would you pay to be introduced to your Love?**
  Connect4Love offers deluxe service

- **Do you need tips and tools or a complete make-over?**
  Connect4love offers personal styling & suggestions

Connect4love is worth it's weight in gold!

Contact us now

www.connect4love.com.au

Offices in:

Singapore - Kuala Lumpur – London - Sydney

Connect4Love

Expensive · Discrete – Personal – Successful – Match-Makers

Happiness is...
a loving relationship

If you have a high profile position and discretion is most important and you don't want anyone knowing your business, then the up market but more expensive option is **Connect4Love.**

They specialise in match-making for the busy high flyers, celebrity, CEO's and millionaires with a fabulous, very confidential service, which includes the organising of restaurants, limousines, flower services, gift services, helicopter flights, weekend getaways and surprise cocktail parties...

They guarantee discretion and very personal service.
Prices range from $1000 to $10,000 – worth it if you find your ideal partner!

Relationship Seminars

Shelley Sykes is a sought after Inspirational Speaker as well as an author and TV Presenter. Her audience laugh and learn about love, luck, looks and lifestyle. She is based in Sydney, yet she speaks around the world at Relationship seminars.

Need a little love in your life?
Take action and become a passionate partner or soul mate magnet.

If you want to organise an event or sponsor Shelley to present her relationship seminars for your company then please contact:

Shelley Sykes
PO Box 452
Concord
Sydney NSW
Australia
T: +61 438 016622
shelley@shelleysykes.com

I'm
Sexy, Single & Ready
to Mingle

I'm
Sexy & Single

I was Sexy & Single
Now I'm
Lucky-in-Love

Lucky-in-Love... and
still **Sexy!**

I'm a
Chick Magnet!

I'm a
Man Magnet!

Beware
Beware
I'M SEXY!

SEXY &
SINGLE

Beware
Beware
I'M SEXY!

Sexy Single T-Shirts

You can purchase on line any of the following T-shirts:

- I'm Sexy, Single & Ready to Mingle
- I'm Sexy & Single ⚥
- I was Sexy & Single Now I'm **Lucky-in-Love**
- **Lucky-in-Love**...and still Sexy
- I'm a Chick Magnet!
- I'm a Man Magnet!
- Beware I'm Sexy
- ⚥ Large logo – Sexy & Single

Colours: Black/White or Pink
Sizes: Small, Medium, Large & Extra Large
Price: $35

www.shelleysykes.com

Happiness Bug
T-Shirts

You can purchase on line any of the following T-shirts:

- Beware Happiness is contagious
- I'm Happy
- I've caught the Happiness Bug (No logo)
- I've caught the Happiness Bug (lge logo)
- I've caught the Happiness Bug (sml logo)
- I've caught the Happiness Bug (centre logo)
- Happy
- Get Syked
- I'm Syked

Colours: Black/White or Pink
Sizes: Small, Medium, Large & Extra Large
Price: $35

www.shelleysykes.com

Happiness
Experience Seminars

Shelley will be conducting seminars around the world to teach the **Happiness Experience** techniques to all those that wish to be able to keep the **Happiness Syndrome** alive and well each day.

Become empowered and make every moment count.

Happiness is an attitude and if you would like to have **The Happiness Experience** each day to achieve your dreams and live your best lives then this seminar is not to be missed.

Ideal for leadership

Presentation Skills

Inter-personal communication skills

Positive Attitude

Personal Development

Book now.

www.shelleysykes.com

Happy Energising Spray

$24.95

www.shelleysykes.com

Happy Energising Spray

Need a little help to lift your mood?

Happy Energising Spray will lift those blues and make you bounce.

Happy Energising Spray is scientifcally proven to raise your vibration. Take the pressure out of concentrated effort, let the essential oils and nutrients lift your aura the natural way, effective immediately.

Price: $24.95

www.shelleysykes.com

The Happiness Bug

'Magic happens despite
your circumstances.
It isn't what happens
to you in life that counts.
It's what you do about it
that matters!'

SHELLEY SYKES

www.shelleysykes.com

The Happiness Bug

'A happy person is a
fulfilled person'

EDWARD DE BONO

www.shelleysykes.com

2B1 Charitable Foundation

If you want to make an active contribution on your journey to faster and greater joy and prosperity...as well as **Make a Difference** log onto

www.2b1charity.org

You can become a regular supporter of our local and international projects such as:

Dolphcomm – sponsoring children and adults with needs to swim with wild dolphins

Step to the Future – teenager leadership skills.

Worldwide Food Organisation – teaching people in starved lands how to become self-sufficient.

Plant a Tree – Helping replenish the trees.

2B1 Sanctuary – a place for children and families to regenerate and revitalise their mind, body and souls.

Wannabee foundation – helping children.

One World – One Planet – One People – 2B1

2B1 Charitable Foundation, PO Box 452, Concord, NSW, 2137, Australia

Relationship Consultancy

Shelley is commissioned to work in a consultancy capacity to support your leadership teams to create and continue **Happy Relations at work.**

- For reduced staff turnover
- Increased profits
- Happier work environments

For further details contact: **shelley@shelleysykes.com**

Corporate Presentation Seminars

For those of you interested in learning the art of pampering yourself and bringing your personality and creating your image to suit the person you are creating, then book to be on one of Shelley's popular style seminars.

1. Learn how to brand yourself and create a non-verbal message.

2. From 'Hats to Heels' and every occasion gain the skills that give you self-esteem and confidence.

3. Heaps of beauty and health tips.

4. Learn how to put your style and personality into your home and reflect the you that you have created and are developing into.

Log onto **www.shelleysykes.com**

View the tips and tools and get a free newsletter:

www.beautifulunlimited.com

WORDS OF INSPIRATION

Shelley Sykes

Words of inspiration is a book filled with daily quotes and a call to action, that will inspire you to follow your own dreams and passions. It can be read sequentially or at random. You always get the right message at the right time!

www.shelleysykes.com

Price: $24.95

Happiness Guru at your next conference

Shelley Sykes known as the 'Happiness Guru', is a charismatic keynote speaker and human potential expert helping Fortune 500 companies build more effective communications between management, staff and customers for win-win scenarios and healthier, happier environments.

If you wish Shelley to speak, entertain and support your corporation then please contact Shelley directly or ask your preferred speakers bureau to contact Shelley.

Phone: +61 438 016622
Email: shelley@shelleysykes.com

www.shelleysykes.com

Books by Shelley Sykes

Sexy Single & Ready to Mingle

This is a recipe for relationships. How to magnetise your soul mate into your life to become **Lucky-in-Loves**. Edward de Bono calls it the Karma Sutra of the mind. $24.95

The Happiness Bug

How to Catch the Happiness Bug and stay con-taminated. Learn how to convert any disaster into a Happy Experience and be happy every day despite your circumstances. Price : $24.95

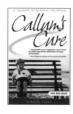

Callum's Cure

Inspirational true life story of Shelley and her quest to be the best person and parent.

Best-seller $24.95

Words of Inspiration

The Happiness Guru has summated all her tips into one book with call to action. This book can be used daily. $24.95

Coming soon...Forever Young & The Road to Wealth.
10% all book sales goes to the 2B1 Charitable Foundation.

www.shelleysykes.com